A Patriot's Guide

Exodus

An EZ Illustrated Commentary Of The Book Of Exodus

Written and illustrated by Jeff Todd

Exodus
An EZ Illustrated Commentary Of The Book Of Exodus

Published by:
Jeff Todd
Newnan, Georgia

ISBN-13: 9798452643548

The purpose of this book is to share the Good News of Jesus Christ and put it out there in an easy-to-understand way. It is part of the outreach ministry of Jeff Todd.

Please note that there will be mistakes and misprints in this book. We are all human, right? We hope you won't find too many of them. This book was edited to the best of the author's ability and he will not be held responsible for errors.

Direct all correspondence to:

A Patriot's Guide c/o Jeff Todd
PO Box 71972
Newnan, GA 30271-1972

www.apatriotsguide.com

Contents

Introduction

The Book of Exodus is the second book of the Bible. It's located in the Old Testament section right after the Book of Genesis. It has

been said that the writer of this book was Moses. Mostly because his name is mentioned a lot and that much of the information in it was given by God to him. That makes sense, so we'll go with it. It was also written between 1450 – 1410 B.C. That's pretty old. That means we will be reading some ancient history. Thankfully, it won't be from an old dusty scroll.

The Book of Exodus begins where the Book of Genesis leaves off. God's people, the Israelites, had become slaves to the Egyptians and cry out to God to free them. God uses a man named Moses to get the job done. After their rescue, God makes a covenant with them and gives them laws to abide by and blueprints on how to build a tabernacle (a holy tent) for worshiping Him. But, none of this was simple. There was definitely more to this story than that. Believe me, I've already read this and there were times when I felt sorry for Moses. He had to deal with some stressful situations. I'm sure he had worries and may have felt like he had too much on his plate. But, God never gives us a job to do without preparing us for it. He will also send people our way to help get the job done.

Exodus is interesting because it gives you some history of Israel. It also gives you some insight on how awesome God is and how he loves His people. The stories in this book offer some action and drama. I can understand why Hollywood created many movies based on it. An example would be the 1956 blockbuster hit, The Ten Commandments, starring Charlton Heston and Yul Brynner. It was a huge success. Another great example would be one of my favorites, The Prince Of Egypt, which was an animated musical movie by DreamWorks that came out in 1998. We still have a copy of this on VHS. Yes, I know. We're probably the only ones in the world that still has VHS movies.

I'll admit, some of Exodus was a little boring. When I started reading about how the tabernacle was to be built and it gave all the specs on how to build it, the details was a little much. I mean, chapters and chapters of details. I kept asking myself, "Why is this even important to know?" But,... keep in mind, these details were from God and that's how God does things. He is very much into details in

everything in life. Everything has a reason and a purpose. He doesn't just slap things together. Am I right?

This guide, that you hold in your hand, is what I received from reading the Book of Exodus. I had some struggles, but I worked them out. I hope it helps you.

Today we are going to begin reading the Book of Exodus from start to finish. If you're reading A Patriot's Guide for the first time, the large bold title at the top middle of some pages are the chapters. The smaller bold titles are what I like to call 'sub chapters'. And the scripture under them is for reference. This will let you know where we are reading from so that we can follow along together. You should find this in your Bible and read it first before reading from this guide.

This should be fun. If you get tired, put it down and start again tomorrow. Let's enjoy the Bible together. That's the way it was intended. Are you ready? Grab your Bible because you will need it. Let's begin...

Israel In Egypt

The Israelites Oppressed
Exodus 1:1 – 1:22

At the end of the Book of Genesis, we learned that Joseph (a descendant of Abraham) was in charge of Pharaoh's stuff. He saved the people by coming up with a plan of storing food before the great famine hit their land. The people were able to eat during a time when there was no food to eat, except for what Joseph had stored up a few years in advance. These people could buy it directly from him – not given for free. As time rolled on, they ran out of money and started bartering. It began with their livestock and eventually they traded their land and their physical bodies in exchange for this food. But, these Hebrews were happy to do it. For them, it was better than starving to death.

These Israelites had become slaves to Pharaoh. But, at the time, it wasn't really as bad as it sounds. These people could still live on their land and continue doing the stuff they did before – things like farming and raising livestock. The only exception was that they really didn't own anything and they had to give a fifth of everything they produced to Pharaoh. This made them a slave and they were cool with it.

The Book of Exodus begins in Chapter 1 (verse 1) by giving us a recap of Jacob and his sons, including his descendants, that were living in Egypt. There was a total of seventy people. From these people, a great multitude of offspring was created. They were busy populating. And there's only one way to populate, right? Well, that's what they did and they did it a lot. According to the verses, they filled the land up and this worried the new Pharaoh that had come to power. He was afraid that if he had ever gone to war, these Israelites would join forces with his enemies and would possibly wipe him out. He had to do something about this 'population' problem. And no, he didn't invent the birth control pill.

He came up with a brilliant idea. He would work them harder. They were his slaves — he owned them — and could do whatever he pleased. He put slave masters in charge of them. Their job was to work them ruthlessly. Maybe they only got 30-minute lunches

and two 15-minute breaks every day. It could be that they had to work mandatory overtime seven days a week. Or maybe they did some corporate restructuring that made one person do two jobs while maintaining quota levels for both. I'm sure they didn't get any 'paid time off'. This could be where we get the term 'slave driver'.

But, the harder they made the Israelites work, the more babies they would produce. I'm not really sure how this was possible, but maybe they found some intimate time on one of their 15-minute breaks. Who knows? It's possible.

The king of Egypt had a talk with two of the Hebrew midwives – Shiphrah and Puah. A midwife was someone that took care of a mother and her newborn baby. In addition to helping the mother in delivery, this midwife would basically fill in by doing motherly things, such as feeding, bathing and changing the baby's poopy diapers. The king gave these two midwives a new assignment to their job description. He wanted them to weed out the Israelite boys by simply killing them as soon as they slid out of the birth canal. Say what?

It sounded like an easy task, but these ladies feared God and didn't do it. Killing a newborn baby back in those days was definitely something you didn't do. Not only was it morally wrong, but you knew God didn't like it either. So, it was a definite no. But, by not obeying the king's orders, these ladies would have some explaining to do. And they did. By telling him that 'Hebrew women pop out babies faster than a midwife can get to them' seemed to be a good enough answer to him. He was cool with that answer.

Because of their faithfulness, God blessed the midwives with families of their own and the Israelites kept on having children. The place was growing out of control. Pharaoh had to come up with another plan to trim the population. This time he told his people to throw every boy that was born into the Nile. Nile? It's a river... that might have big sea creatures in it like crocodiles and man-eating catfish. If the newborn babies didn't drown first, they might just get eaten alive. Either way, Pharaoh would accomplish his goal.

The Birth Of Moses
Exodus 2:1 – 2:10

A man of the house of Levi marries a Levite woman and they have a newborn son. Instead of allowing this child to be thrown into the Nile, she decided to hide him for three months. I'm sure this was illegal because she knew good and well that Pharaoh wanted all of the newborn Hebrew baby boys to be thrown in the Nile. It was like the law and this woman was breaking it.

Finally, it got to the point to where she couldn't hide him any longer. I can only assume that this child had a nice set of lungs and probably made loud screeching noises when he cried. This would have blown their cover. So, she decided to build him a 'baby boat' out of papyrus and coated it with tar and pitch so that it wouldn't sink. She then put the baby in it and placed it among the reeds that were along the banks of the Nile. The baby's sister stood nearby to see what would happen to him.

Pharaoh's daughter went down to the Nile to take a bath. Maybe they didn't have indoor plumbing yet or that bath tubs were still in the 'creation' phase. I can only imagine how 'not clean' you would feel by taking a nice cold bath in a muddy river. But hey, whatever. Pharaoh's daughter saw the papyrus basket in the reeds and told her slave girl to go get it. When she opened the basket, she saw the baby. The kid was crying and it made her feel sorry for it. I guess the annoying sound of a crying baby or the prune look a baby gives when it cries touched her heart strings. One thing is for sure, she knew it was a Hebrew baby. According to Pharaoh, we know where Hebrew babies belong. His daughter didn't get the memo and took the baby as her own.

Here's where it gets tricky. The baby's sister walks up to Pharaoh's daughter and asks her, "Shall I go get a Hebrew woman to come and nurse the baby for you?"

Pharaoh's daughter replies, "Yes, go."

The baby's sister goes and gets the baby's 'real' mother (which is her mother, too). The 'real' mother ends up nursing the child (her own child) and Pharaoh's daughter pays her to do it. Ain't that weird and kind of cool?

When the child got older, the 'real' mother gives the child to Pharaoh's daughter and he becomes her son. She names him Moses. I assume his name means 'drawn out of water'.

Moses Flees To Midian
Exodus 2:11 – 2:25

Nothing is said here about Moses' childhood. He goes from being the son of Pharaoh's daughter at 3 months old and now he is grown. We know he grew up in royalty and can only imagine what that would have been like. He may have had the finer things in life. He could have worn fancy designer clothes made from real camel hair and maybe he  had the latest techno-gadgets that were popular with the rich kids (such as the sun dial wrist watch or a state-of-the-art calculator known as the abacus). I'm sure he had it made in the shade and lived the good life.

One day he decided to go out where his own people were working. He saw the rough labor conditions. He also saw an Egyptian beating a Hebrew. Remember, Moses was born a Hebrew and lived as an Egyptian. So, I don't know if Moses was showing pity as an Egyptian man or he was upset because an Egyptian was beating one of his own people. The verses tell me that Moses knew the Hebrew person was being mistreated and decided to do something about it. He waited for the right moment when no one was around and killed the Egyptian. He hid his body in the sand.

Later, Moses saw two Hebrews fighting. He stopped them and questioned them about it. One of the men got offended and asked Moses if he planned to kill them like he did the Egyptian. Uh oh! Moses became afraid because he thought nobody knew what he had done. Moses was a murderer and now he had an eyewitness. What was he going to do?

The news made it's way to Pharaoh. When Pharaoh found out about what Moses had done, he tried to kill him. Maybe this was a punishment for his crimes. Moses was forced to become a fugitive and went to live in Midian. He was now a wanted man.

15

There was a priest of Midian named Reuel. He had seven daughters. Moses was hanging out at a well in Midian when Reuel's daughters showed up to get water for his flocks. Also, coming to the well, were shepherds. They tried to run the daughters off from the well, but Moses stood up and came to their rescue. Did Moses beat up a bunch of local shepherds that day? It doesn't say, but it would have been cool. It could have been like a scene from a Chuck Norris movie where Moses does a cool roundhouse kick that knocked the shepherds unconscious. That would have been awesome. All I know is that he drew water for the seven daughters. This led into a personal invitation by their father to come eat at his house. I guess he was impressed with Moses' bravery for protecting his daughters that he decided to feed him. I think he also gave him a place to live. But, one thing is for sure, Reuel gave Moses one of his daughters to marry. Her name was Zipporah. Together they had a son that Moses named Gershom. I hope all of this didn't happen in one day. I'm sure it didn't.

A long time had passed. The king of Egypt had died. The Israelites were tired of being sick and tired. This 'slavery thing' was too much, so they cried out to God. God heard them and was concerned for their well-being. God also remembered His covenant with Abraham, Isaac and Jacob. You know, the one about the Promised Land. Something good is about to happen.

Moses And The Burning Bush
Exodus 3:1 – 3:21

Moses was tending to his father-inlaw's flock... uh oh!... newsflash!... we have a name change. OK... Moses' father-inlaw ... his old name was Reuel. Now it is Jethro. Jethro? What happened? Did he get a dose of some hillbilly sipping sauce or something? The name Jethro is like the most 'hillbilliest' name you can think of. It's like slang for 'Jeff' or 'Jeffrey'. Hey! Wait! That's my name.

Anyway, Moses is outside tending to Jethro's flock. He leads the flock to the far side of the desert and came to Horeb (the mountain of God). It was there that the angel of the Lord appeared to Moses. It was in the form of 'fire within a bush'. Moses noticed that the bush didn't burn up even though a fire was burning inside it. This caught his attention so he walked a little closer. This was when God spoke to Moses.

There was a quite a bit of conversation going on between God and Moses at the burning bush. Here's a few highlights that I thought were pretty interesting:

- Moses couldn't come any closer to the burning bush. Actually, he was told to take his sandals off because he was standing on holy ground.
- Moses hid his face because he was afraid to look at God.

- God gave Moses a special assignment. He was to go to Pharaoh and bring God's people (the Israelites) out of Egypt.
- Moses had doubts about himself. It didn't sink in that God would be working through him.
- When Moses asked God who he should tell the Pharaoh that sent him, God gave a few names: I AM WHO I AM, I AM, Lord, God of your fathers, God of Abraham, God of Isaac and God of Jacob.
- Moses had to assemble the elders of Israel and tell them what God had planned to do.

It sounds like God will be doing the work and Moses will basically be the voice. Also, from what I've read, it sounds like Moses would be up against some obstacles. But, as soon as God performs some 'wonders' for Pharaoh, he will gladly let them go. Actually, it mentions that the Egyptians will give Moses and the Israelites some parting gifts (such as silver and gold) as they journey on out of there. I think this was God's way of giving Moses permission to plunder the Egyptians.

Signs For Moses
Exodus 4:1 – 4:17

Moses was unsure of this assignment that God had given him. He had doubts about himself and in his abilities to make this task possible. Even though God told him to do this assignment, I don't think he fully understood that God would be doing all of this through him. He had 'what ifs'.

What if they don't believe me or listen to me?

This is similar to how we may feel when God is telling us to do something for Him. We may realize how inadequate we are for the job. It's probably true. We may not be able to do that 'thing' in our own strength. But, if God is sending you to it, He will give you everything you need to accomplish it.

To help build Moses' confidence, God shows Moses some signs that would help him realize that He would be with him on his journey. The first sign was with the staff that Moses had in his hand. God told him to throw it on the ground. When he did, God turned it into a snake. This scared the stew out of Moses so he ran from it. The funny thing is that Moses had to go back and pick it up by it's tail. Can you imagine how hard that would have been to do? But, Moses did it. And when he did, the snake turned back into a staff.

The next sign was with the cloak that Moses was wearing. God told him to stick his hand inside the cloak. And when he pulled it back out, it was leprous. This was some kind of serious infection with sores and rotting flesh caused by bacteria. I imagine it was gross. It probably freaked Moses out. God told him to put his hand back into the cloak. Moses did, and when he pulled his hand out again, his hand was restored. It was as if nothing ever happened. I'm sure Moses was freaked out and amazed.

It seems that Moses will be sharing these signs with the Egyptians when he arrives. God tells him, that if they don't believe these two signs, to go to the Nile and get some water and pour it on the ground. This water would turn to blood.

Moses made an attempt to get out of doing this mission. He reminded God of how slow he was in speech and tongue. He may have had a stuttering problem. He could have been Southern because everybody knows how slow we talk in the South. God tried to comfort him. He let him know that He would help him speak and teach him what to say. Moses still didn't want to do this.

"God, please send someone else to do it." Moses said.

God was getting angry. Instead of smashing Moses like a bug, He remembered Moses' brother, Aaron. Aaron was a good speaker. God assigned the 'speaking job' to him. All Moses had to do was tell him the news. Together, they would go to Egypt and tell Pharaoh to let their people go. God would be giving them the words to say. It should be a quick 'in and out' kind of thing. Easy peasy, right? I seriously doubt it.

In verse 17, God tells Moses to take a very important item with him – his staff. This thing would be used on numerous occasions where miraculous signs would be needed. I hope he remembers to take it.

Moses Returns To Egypt
Exodus 4:18 – 4:31

Moses, who was married with children, had been living with his father-inlaw (Jethro). He was a fugitive (maybe running from the law) because he had murdered an Egyptian back when he was living in Pharaoh's house in Egypt. Many years had probably passed and now it was time for Moses to leave. Moses accepted the assignment that God had given him.

While Moses was in Midian, God assured him that it was safe to go to Egypt. All of the men that wanted to kill him for the crime he committed were now dead. The 'coast was clear' and it was now safe for Moses to return to Egypt. Moses told Jethro about his plans and loaded up the donkey. He took his wife (Zipporah) and their sons. I'm sure they took along their clothes and things they needed for their travel. Moses definitely took his staff because, according to God, he would be using it a lot. It would actually be the first thing he would use when he arrived in Egypt. God told him to use it for performing all of the wonders he had been shown before Pharaoh. That's how he would know that Moses was 'God sent'.

Moses knew Pharaoh would have a hardened heart way before he got there because God planned it that way. Basically, Moses would tell Pharaoh to 'let my people go' and the reply would be 'no'. Moses already knew this ahead of time but still went through the motions. The verses say that God hardened the Pharaoh's heart. Why did God harden the Pharaoh's heart?

Pharaoh was an evil man and already had a hardened heart. Think about it. He probably had over a million Israelite slaves that he treated badly. Plus, he was killing all of their newborn sons. What kind of person would do this? Sounds like someone with no heart at all.

God could have just passed judgment on Pharaoh and everyone in Egypt. It would have been easier to just wipe them all out. But he didn't. There was a bigger picture. There were things that God wanted to show the Israelites and the Egyptians. He wanted to show them all why He is mighty and merciful. By hardening Pharaoh's heart was simply making it harder than it already was. This probably kept Pharaoh from altering the big plan God had in store for them all.

22

God wanted Moses to go to the Pharaoh and tell him to let the Israelites go. Moses knew ahead of time that Pharaoh would say 'no'. The next step would be for Moses to warn him that his firstborn would die because of his response. Keep in mind, these things haven't happened yet. It like God was giving Moses a 'heads up' on what was about to happen. He was preparing him for the assignment. That's what God does.

If God calls you to do something for Him, He will prepare you for it. That's also how you can tell if what you're doing for God is actually what God wants you to do. Did He prepare you for it? If not, then it's probably not a God-called assignment. It's time to step down. Know what I'm saying?

Verse 24 sounded kind of strange. God was about to kill Moses. Thankfully, Zipporah (Moses' wife) had a knife. She circumcised her son and slaps the foreskin on Moses' feet. Moses was free to continue living. To me, that's weird. What's that all about? Here's what I found out:

God had a covenant with Israel. Part of that covenant was a law that stated that all males would be circumcised. If not, they and their families would be removed from God's blessings. Moses hadn't done this yet. I guess living in Pharaoh's house for so long had made him forget the law. It's a good thing his wife remembered and carried a knife. Now Moses could be the message deliverer that God intended him to be.

Moses meets up with his brother, Aaron. He explains everything that God had told him. They both, in turn, meet up with the elders and they share the details again. Everyone was excited that God had heard their prayers. Something was about to get done. Finally! Four hundred years was a long time to wait for an answered prayer. But, that day, they got the great news. It made them want to bow down and worship God.

Bricks Without Straw
Exodus 5:1 – 5:21

Moses and Aaron did as God instructed them. They went to see Pharaoh. They told him what God had wanted him to hear: TO LET HIS PEOPLE GO. But, Pharaoh refused. The whole 'letting go' thing wasn't something of any interest to him. He had a problem with it:

- Pharaoh didn't know God, so he felt like he didn't have to do what He said.
- There were a lot of Israelite slaves. I've read that maybe there were almost two million of them. Letting them go would have created a major decrease in labor productivity. It could shut down the whole brick-laying operation. Who would have been left to build those cool pyramids? For the record, Walmart currently has a little over two million employees. 'Letting go' for Pharaoh would be similar to closing Walmart down worldwide. Can you imagine that?

Pharaoh must have been offended at Moses and Aaron for delivering such a silly request. If the Israelite slaves were whining about their working conditions, Pharaoh felt like they were being lazy and must have had too much time on their hands. It was time to give them more things to do.

Pharaoh had a meeting with his slave drivers and the Israelite foremen. Instead of supplying the slaves with straw to make bricks, the slaves would now have to gather their own straw while maintaining their current production levels. This was double work and an impossibility.

The foremen were beaten for the slaves lack of production over a two-day period. They were down in numbers – less bricks were being produced. The slave drivers wanted to know why? The foremen knew the answer and went to Pharaoh to explain. They hoped he would be more understanding. But, no. He wanted them to still meet the quota and blamed the problem on their laziness.

The Israelite slaves and foremen were stressed. Everything was fine until Moses and Aaron showed up. The same two guys that they considered heroes and God's deliverers in the beginning were now causing a stink in their lives. They didn't like it. At this point, I bet they wished Moses and Aaron had left well enough alone.

God Promises Deliverance
Exodus 5:22 – 6:12

Moses had questions. I'm sure many of us have been in a situation like this. We do what we feel like God is telling us, yet the results don't turn out like we expected them. Many times they turn out worse. This was the feeling that Moses was experiencing. He wanted to know 'why', so he asked God about it.

God's reply was one of encouragement. He assured Moses that He would do as He promised. Pharaoh would let His people go. The Israelites would get a firsthand experience in seeing Him follow through with His promise. It would be presented in a big way - in a way that they would never forget.

God told Moses to relay the message to the Israelites. So, he did. Unfortunately, they didn't believe a word of it. They were discouraged and maybe they felt a little betrayed by God. God also told Moses to go back to Pharaoh and tell him again to 'let His people go'. I don't think Moses wanted to because he already knew what Pharaoh would say. To him, it was like 'what's the point'. I imagine Moses was also discouraged about the rescue mission, too.

Family Record Of Moses And Aaron
Exodus 6:13 – 6:27

I think the purpose of these verses is add a little bit of clarification on who Aaron and Moses were. Back in the day, there could have been several fellas out there with the same name. That's how it is in present day, too. How many people would you think shared your name? Some names are just more popular than others.

Clans of Reuben (firstborn son of Israel)

- Hanoch
- Pallu
- Hezron
- Carmi

Clans of Simeon

- Jemuel
- Jamin
- Ohad
- Jakin
- Zohar
- Shaul (son of a Canaanite woman)

Clans of Levi (lived 137 years)

- Gershon
  - Libni
  - Shimei
- Kohath (lived 133 years)
  - Amram (married his father's sister, Jochebed. Lived 137 years)
    - Aaron (married Elisheba)
      - Nadab
      - Abihu
      - Eleazar (married a daughter of Putiel)
        - Phinehas
      - Ithamar
    - Moses
  - Izhar
    - Korah (the Korahite clan)
      - Assir
      - Elkanah
      - Abiasaph
    - Nepheg

- ■ Zicri
  - ○ Hebron
  - ○ Uzziel
    - ■ Mishael
    - ■ Elzaphan
    - ■ Sithri
- • Merari
  - ○ Mahli
  - ○ Mushi

HERE'S THE LATEST FOR THE 21ST CENTURY...

POPULAR BABY NAMES FROM THE OLD TESTAMENT

BABY NAMES ENTHUSIASTS

Most of the names mentioned above are probably not as popular as they were back in the day. Other than Moses and Aaron, I have never heard any of them from where I'm from. But, who knows? They may come back in style again.

Another interesting thing I saw from this list was that a man named Amram married his Aunt Jochebed. Yes, I know. It sounded weird. This wasn't uncommon back then, even though today it would be considered 'incest'. There wasn't a law yet that forbid it. But, it turned out to be a good thing that this relationship happened. Without it, Aaron and Moses would have never been born.

Aaron To Speak For Moses
Exodus 6:28 – 7:7

We learned from Exodus 4: 10 that Moses had some type of speech impediment. He was a slow talker.

And Moses said unto the Lord, O my Lord, I am not eloquent, neither heretofore, nor since thou hast spoken unto thy servant: but I am slow of speech, and of a slow tongue. - Exodus 4: 10

And now from Exodus 6: 12 and 6:30, we learn something new about Moses' oral handicap.

And Moses spake before the Lord, saying, Behold, the children of Israel have not hearkened unto me; how then shall Pharaoh hear me, who am of uncircumcised lips? - Exodus 6: 12

And Moses said before the Lord, Behold, I am of uncircumcised lips, and how shall Pharaoh hearken unto me? - Exodus 6: 30

Uncircumcised lips? I'm reading this from the King James Version. Other versions use different wording and simply say it means that he was basically a poor speaker. But, why didn't Moses just say 'I am slow of speech and tongue'

like he did before in Exodus 4: 10? There has to be a deeper meaning.

We have learned that a male in those days would get circumcised to show that he was part of God's family. To be uncircumcised would mean the opposite. Maybe Moses felt like the words that would be coming from his mouth would not be from God. Maybe he thought he was really doing all of this 'in his own strength' and that God wasn't in it. He may have thought that if it was 'of God', then Pharaoh would have automatically said 'go ahead and let them go' on the first attempt. That would mean that Moses had doubts about God working through him in the whole mission. That makes sense to me.

AAH!

OOH!

THE LEWIS GUIDE READERS

The following verses is where God had to explain how the process will work and, of course, told him everything that he needed to say to Pharaoh. This is important because we're dealing with a man that thought he himself was a god. I'm talking about Pharaoh. He placed himself on a pedestal above everyone else. I'm sure he thought he was better than everybody and felt like they needed to be answering to him. So, if someone like Moses walks up to him, he automatically will look down on them and devalue anything that comes out of their mouth. God wanted Moses to walk in with authority; as if he owned the place. Not only did Moses need to know that God was working through him, he also wanted him to act like it.

This could apply to us that serve God. We don't need to appear to be anything less than a child of the King. We should hold our heads up high and be bold with our words to others, especially when we are delivering an important message (the Gospel).

Moses was eighty and his brother, Aaron, was eighty-three when they were facing Pharaoh. They were just a couple of old guys with an important message.

Aaron's Staff Becomes A Snake
Exodus 7:8 – 7:13

The verses are pretty much self-explanatory. It sounded like a competition between Aaron and his staff against Pharaoh's magicians and their walking sticks. The result was that all of them turned into snakes, but Aaron's swallowed theirs whole.

This was one of the signs that God shared with Moses back in Chapter 4 of how to turn his staff into a snake. Also, now in verse 9, God tells Moses when and how he will be applying this sign. It's like God is helping Moses and Aaron through every step of the way.

Even after seeing this awesome miracle, Pharaoh's heart was still hard and wouldn't listen. The pages were unfolding just like God had said.

The Plague Of Blood
Exodus 7:14 – 7:24

If the snake trick didn't get Pharaoh's attention, maybe a few plagues will. This is the first of ten plagues that God sent down to Pharaoh and the land of Egypt.

As Pharaoh was walking to the Nile in the morning to get a drink of water... STOP! For the record, people from back in the day had to walk to get water. Bottled water and indoor plumbing had not been invented yet. Let's just hope they didn't use the bathroom and drink from the same water hole. Anyway, back to the story...

As Pharaoh was walking to the Nile in the morning to get a drink of water, Moses and Aaron were standing at the banks to greet him. They gave him a 'heads up' of what was about to happen and then proceeded to follow through.

Aaron held the staff in his hand above all of the water in Egypt – the ponds, streams, canals and reservoirs. All of it turned to blood. This included all of the water that they had stored in wooden buckets and jars. By doing this, they couldn't drink from it. It wasn't drinkable. To make things worse, it made the whole area stink because all of the fish that were living in it had died. Have you ever smelled fish that has been dead for a while? It's not good at all. Here's a quick story...

A few years ago in our business, we had the opportunity to clean out a home that had been foreclosed on by the bank. The person that lived in this house was a business owner and I assume his business went sour. His business was a fish market business. That means this man bought, prepared and sold fish from his house. Well, when the bank foreclosed on his house, he left a lot of his personal belongings behind. This included refrigerators, freezers and a sink full of fish he was preparing before he got the bad news from the bank. When he left, the power company also shut off his electricity and the house set for months. Now we had the wonderful opportunity to clean this mess up. Everything smelled like dead rotting fish. It made us gag and the smell went through my nose and landed on my taste buds. I could taste it! This terrible smell stayed in my lungs for several days. It was one of the worst experiences of my life.

Pharaoh wasn't impressed with the bloody Nile or the smelly fish. I think he was more concerned about the 'magic trick' than the fact that his people would now be struggling to find drinkable water. The verses say that he even had his magicians to perform the same miracle. This would mean the Pharaoh was looking for ways to outperform God. It had more to do about 'supreme power' – Pharaoh against God. He will find out soon enough.

The Plague Of Frogs
Exodus 7:25 – 8:15

It had been seven days since the last plague. Moses made another attempt to get Pharaoh to let the Israelites go. This time,

after he had said no, Aaron stretched his hand over the waters and frogs started coming from everywhere. They quickly populated Egypt and began getting into their homes, beds, ovens and kneading troughs. They were all over the place. Pharaoh had his magicians perform a trick that did the same. This time, I think the plague caught his attention.

Can you imagine how it would be to have a frog infestation? I'm not talking about just a few frogs. You know how we act when we are swimming in a pool at night and a couple of frogs hop in with us? Imagine swimming in a pool of frogs! Or how about not being able to walk because frogs are everywhere? All it would take is one wrong step and... SQUISH!! It would be annoying and a bit freaky.

Pharaoh called for Moses and Aaron. He was willing to make a deal. He said if they would pray to God to get rid of the frogs, he would let His people go. They agreed. The next day, Moses and Aaron did as they said and the frogs died right where they were. The place started stinking again from the smell of rotting frogs. Now it was Pharaoh's turn to fulfill his part of the bargain. But, no. Pharaoh lied and didn't let God's people go. He was just a liar with a hard heart.

The Plague Of Gnats
Exodus 8:16 – 8:19

Aaron stretched out the staff and struck the dust of the ground in Egypt. The dust became gnats and were all over the place. The magicians made an attempt to perform the same miracle and couldn't. They told Pharaoh that this was truly an act of God. Pharaoh still had a hard heart and wouldn't listen.

There are people out there that don't believe in God. They don't believe He exists and that the people that do believe in Him are nuttier than squirrel terds. Some non-believers will say that they would believe if they could see a sign or a miracle. If they could 'see', then they would 'believe'. Here we have a man (Pharaoh) that got a chance to witness a God-given miracle. He even had his trusted companions telling him that the miracle was from God, but Pharaoh chose not to believe anyway. He was stubborn, hard-headed and spiritually blind.

If you're a non-believer reading this today, look around you. You are surrounded by 'miracle' proof that God exists. It's easier for you to just dismiss it and move on. Maybe... maybe you're just stubborn.

The Plague Of Flies
Exodus 8:20 – 8:32

God instructed Moses to get up early in the morning and confront Pharaoh. He was to tell him to 'let God's people go'. If Pharaoh refused, God wanted him to know that He would be sending him some unwanted flying visitors that would populate quickly on the land of Egypt. But, this time, God wouldn't send these flies to Goshen. This was where His people lived and He wanted them to know that He was there with them. This plague would occur the next day.

Just as God had said, the plaque of flies was happening. They were everywhere – in Pharaoh's palace, in his official's homes and throughout the land of Egypt. And no one owned an electric bug zapper. Those weren't invented yet. Everything was ruined by the flies. Pharaoh wasn't too happy about it.

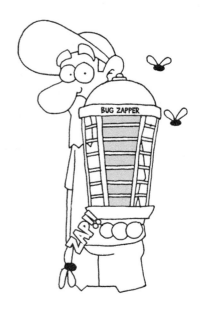

Pharaoh summoned Moses and Aaron. He wanted something done right away. He offered to let them take the Israelites and make their sacrifice to God right there in the land where they were at. It would be quick, both parties would be happy and everyone could go back to work when it was done. Moses didn't think this was a good idea. Moses preferred a three-day trip to the desert to make this sacrifice. Their sacrifice would have been offensive to the Egyptians if they did it right there in front of them. It could have caused a mob of angry Egyptians to stone them to death, so the three-day trip was safer. Pharaoh agreed, but wanted them to hurry up about it. I'm sure he didn't want to hold up production on the brick assembly line. In trade, Moses would have to pray to God to get these flies gone. Moses had doubts that Pharaoh would hold up to his side of the bargain.

You know, I'm beginning to think that, each time Moses tells Pharaoh to 'let the Israelites go', Pharaoh is thinking that it's just for three days so that they can make a sacrifice to God in the desert. After that, they would return and everything would go back to normal. But, if that was the case, why would Pharaoh be so reluctant to 'let them go'? I mean, every time he says 'no', he would get another plague. Maybe deep inside he knows that he would lose them forever.

Pharaoh agrees to the deal that he and Moses made. Moses prays to God to remove the flies. God answers and the flies leave. But, Pharaoh lied once more. He didn't let the people go.

The Plague On Livestock
Exodus 9:1 – 9:7

Per God's request, Moses made another attempt to convince Pharaoh to let God's people go. If Pharaoh said 'no' this time, God would send a plague that would kill all of the livestock (horses, donkeys, camels, cattle, sheep and goats) that belonged to the Egyptians. However, this plague would not affect the livestock of the Israelites. This plague would begin the very next day.

Wanna guess Pharaoh's reply when told, "Let God's people go."?

Yep... it was a 'no'.

The plague happened just as God said. I guess Pharaoh needed further proof and had investigators to go out and check on the livestock. Yep! Only the dead ones belonged to Egypt.

The Plague Of Boils
Exodus 9:8 – 9:12

God told Moses to take handfuls of soot from a furnace and throw it into the air in front of Pharaoh. It would become fine dust that would cover the whole land of Egypt. Boils would break out and form on all of the men and animals throughout the land.

Boils are red, painful, pus-filled bumps that form under the skin. It's similar to what you get on your back-side when you sit for long periods of time. It's like a mega-pimple. People these days like to share videos of people with boils as they mash the white gunk out of them on social networking sites. It's painful and gross. Egypt was getting them all over their body.

All of this didn't phase Pharaoh. He was still saying 'no'.

The Plague Of Hail
Exodus 9:13 – 9:35

This time God sent a major light show from the sky that included thunder, lightning and hail. It was severe. It was the worst that Egypt had ever seen. God told Moses to give Pharaoh a warning. He told him ahead time to place his people and animals in shelter from the storm. Anyone or anything left outside would die.

The storm left a mess. It destroyed everything growing in the fields and 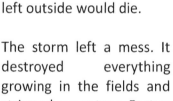 stripped every tree. Fortunately, the only place it did not hail was on the land of Goshen where the Israelites lived.

From Verse 27, I think Pharaoh had a change of heart. He admitted that he had sinned and that God was in the right. He was willing to let the Israelites go as long as Moses prayed the storm away. So, Moses prayed and the storm ceased. Pharaoh was a happy camper, but his heart was still just as hard as it was in the beginning. He, once again, refused to let the Israelites go.

The Plague Of Locusts
Exodus 10:1 – 10:20

Through these plagues, God was revealing Himself to Moses and to the Israelites. It was more than just setting them free. It was a strong message of love for them. They would be able to share this testimony with their generations to come.

This plague was devastating. Whatever crops the Egyptians had left from the hailstorm, these locusts would finish doing the job. God sent enough locusts to cover the entire land of Egypt. Pharaoh's officials were tired and wanted him to surrender. They didn't have much left. The plagues were destroying Egypt right before their very eyes.

Pharaoh finally gives in and tells Moses and Aaron to take their people to go worship their God. But he had one question: "Who all would be going?" Maybe he was concerned about the brick-making assembly line. The production would drop drastically. Who would be left to make them bricks?

Moses told him he would basically be taking everyone with him, including their flocks and herds. Pharaoh didn't like this idea and wanted to bargain. Pharaoh only agreed to allow the men to go with him. The women and animals would have to stay behind. After Pharaoh gave his agreement details, he sent Moses and

Aaron on their way. A compromise like this was not acceptable, so Moses continued with God's plan.

Moses stretched out his staff over Egypt and God made an east wind blow across the land day and night. By morning the next day, the locusts had arrived. They covered Egypt in great numbers. The ground was black and they ate everything in sight.

Pharaoh panicked and quickly called for Moses and Aaron. He realized that he had sinned against God and wanted them to forgive him. He also wanted them to pray and get the pesky locusts removed. Moses did and God sent a very strong west wind. The locusts got caught up in the wind and landed in the Red Sea. They were finally gone – every last one.

You would think that Pharaoh would have a change of attitude by now. Right? But, no. He was still saying 'no'.

The Plague Of Darkness
Exodus 10:21 – 10:29

God told Moses to stretch his hand towards the sky. This created a darkness to cover the land of Egypt for three days. But, it wasn't just your normal everyday darkness either. It doesn't sound like the kind that you create when you cut the light switch off in your bedroom. The verse says, 'darkness that can be felt'. What kind of darkness can be felt?

The only thing that comes to my mind is a 'spiritual' darkness. We have heard from the Bible that God is light.

This then is the message which we have heard of him, and declare unto you, that God is light, and in him is no darkness at all. - 1 John 1: 5

To be separated from Him would leave a person in darkness... spiritual darkness. Maybe that's the issue in this plague. Egypt was in darkness because God was no longer there. They were blind and couldn't see each other or move.

Pharaoh, once again, called out to Moses. This plague had become too much. He wanted Moses to know that he could now let the Israelites go. This included the women and children, but not their flocks and herds. The animals had to stay behind, but Moses needed them for their sacrifice to God. This made Pharaoh mad. He didn't want to see Moses' face again, so he demanded him to leave his presence. If he saw him again, he would kill him.

Moses said, "Aight then." Pharaoh continued with his hardened heart and didn't let the Israelites go.

The Plague On The Firstborn
Exodus 11:1 – 11:10

This was the last plague that God sent to Pharaoh and the land of Egypt. This one would seal the deal. Pharaoh would let God's people go after receiving this one. God guaranteed it.

The sad thing about this plague is that it affected the innocent children of Egypt. The firstborn son of everyone living there would die at midnight. In addition, the firstborn of the cattle would die, too. It would be a very sad event. People in every house would be balling their eyes out in tears. Death would be everywhere.

Before the plague hit, Moses told his people (both men and women) to ask their Egyptian neighbors for items made from silver and gold. It seems that God fixed it so that they would freely give these things to them. This stuff would be used as money to help them along their journey as they left Egypt.

The Passover
Exodus 12:1 – 12:30

Passover, as we probably already know, is a Jewish festival that celebrates the exodus from Egypt and the Israelites' freedom from slavery to the Egyptians. Commemorations today involve a special meal called the Seder, that includes unleavened bread and other food items symbolic of various aspects of the exodus. Passover takes place in the spring, during the Hebrew month of Nisan. In Western countries, Passover is celebrated in early-to mid-April and is always close to Easter. These verses tell us when this all began.

God tells Moses and Aaron to share the news with the Israelites to take a lamb for each household on this special occasion. If a family is too small for one whole lamb, they can share with their neighbor. This lamb must be a year old male lamb without any defects. They will take the lamb on the tenth of the month, take care of it and slaughter it on the fourteenth at twilight. They will take some of the blood from the slaughter and smear it on the sides and tops of the doorways of their home. That same night, they are to eat the meat roasted over a fire mixed with bitter herbs and bread made without yeast. They could not eat the meat raw and there could not be any leftovers. If there were, they had to burn it. Even eating it had instructions. They were to eat with their cloaks tucked under their belts, sandals on their feet with their staff in their hand. They had to eat it in a hurry as if they hadn't ate in days.

On the same night, God would 'pass' through Egypt and strike down every firstborn – both of men and animals. He would bring judgment on the gods of Egypt. When God sees the blood on the doorways, He will 'pass over' it and spare the firstborn life inside. He will then move on to the next house.

This day will be remembered for many generations to come. It will be celebrated as a festival to God every year. This festival will last for seven days and bread without yeast would be eaten every day. The first and seventh day would be treated as a sacred ceremony. No one can work on these two days, except to prepare food for everyone.

From the fourteenth day to the twenty-first, they are to celebrate the Feast of Unleavened Bread. They are to only eat bread made without yeast. Actually, they aren't allowed to have any bread with yeast in their homes.

Midnight came and God did as He said He would. He struck all of the firstborn in Egypt. It didn't matter what your financial status was. If you had a firstborn son, you were a target. It was a sad night for the Egyptians. Every house had a death inside. Can you imagine what that was like?

God sent ten plagues to Egypt to get Pharaoh's attention. Was there more to them? Was He only trying to get Pharaoh's attention to let the Israelites go? Or did He have a message for Egypt, too? From verse 12, I get the impression that God had something to say to the gods they were worshiping as well. Maybe the Israelites were dabbling into the same religious practices as the Egyptians. I mean, they had been living with them for over four hundred years. I imagine it would rub off on them.

I dug deep into the possible meanings of these plagues and borrowed this from the Internet:

The story of the ten plagues that God brought down upon ancient Egypt in Exodus 7 is one of the Old Testament's most famous and dramatic. We normally think of the purpose of these plagues as God's way of demonstrating his power to the Pharaoh and forcing him to release the Hebrew people from slavery. This is certainly true, but there are at least two other reasons for the ten plagues.

Ancient Egypt was a nation that worshiped many gods. They had over one hundred major gods that were interwoven into their culture and daily lives. Since the Hebrew people had lived in Egypt for over four hundred years, they too worshiped these gods.

The Lord was about to have Moses lead the Hebrews out of slavery and into the wilderness to worship and follow Him to the promised land. It is a logical first step to demonstrate to everyone, that He is, in fact, the true God, and that these Egyptian deities are fiction and powerless.

The ten plagues, therefore, were demonstrations of God's absolute power over the Egyptian gods, and proof that they were unable to protect or harm the Hebrew people in any way.

For I will pass through the land of Egypt this night, and will smite all the firstborn in the land of Egypt, both man and beast; and against all the gods of Egypt I will execute judgment: I am the LORD. - Exodus 12: 12

Let's take a look at the ten plagues in Exodus 7, as well as the Egyptian god or gods that were proven to be powerless by each particular plague.

- **First Plague** - The Nile River is turned into blood. As a result, it is undrinkable, putrid, and all the fish die. Apis and Isis, the god and goddess of the Nile, and Khnum, the protector god of the Nile, were shown to be powerless.
- **Second Plague** - Frogs leave the Nile and infest the entire country, then die and completely stink up everything. Heqet is the Egyptian goddess of life and fertility, and is depicted as a woman with the head of a frog. Frogs were considered sacred, and it was forbidden to kill them, but the plague caused millions of them to die.
- **Third Plague** - Aaron struck the dust of the ground with his staff, and the dust turned into gnats which multiplied and spread all over the land and greatly afflicted both man and beast. Geb was the god of earth and soil, and he did nothing to intervene.
- **Fourth Plague** - Great swarms of flies dominated everything, except where the Hebrews lived. Khepri was the Egyptian god of creation and sun movement, and was pictured with the head of a fly. The buzz was that Khepri failed to save the Egyptians from this invasion of his likenesses.
- **Fifth Plague** - All the Egyptian cattle and livestock were infected with a deadly disease. Hathor, the goddess of love who looked like a cow, couldn't help her bovine relatives.
- **Sixth Plague** - All the Egyptian people and animals were inflicted with debilitating boils. Sekhmet, the lioness goddess of healing, didn't cure anyone of this painful condition.
- **Seventh Plague** - Thunder and gigantic hail with fire rains down on all the Egyptians that do not heed Moses' warning. Almost all the crops are lost. Seth, the evil god of storms, sporting the head of an aardvark, can't stop this storm.

- **Eighth Plague** - Huge swarms of locusts polish off the crops of the Egyptians that the hail didn't destroy. Osiris, the green skinned god with mummy wrapped legs, was the god of crop fertility and he couldn't save them.
- **Ninth Plague** - The Egyptians were cast into three days of oppressive darkness. Ra, the great god of the Sun, was unable to shed any light on the matter.
- **Tenth Plague** - The first born of the Pharaoh, as well as the first born of all men and beasts die, except for the Hebrews who follow Moses instructions to keep safe. Pharaoh, who is a man and a god, is unable to prevent the deaths and finally gives the Hebrews their freedom.

The point of all this is that God is a jealous God, and takes sin very seriously. With the plagues in mind, let's read the first commandment from Exodus 20: 2, 3:

I am the LORD thy God, which have brought thee out of the land of Egypt, out of the house of bondage. Thou shalt have no other gods before me. - Exodus 20: 2, 3

God used the ten plagues to expose the Egyptian deities as frauds. There is no doubt that the Hebrew people got the message. It is very probable that many of the Egyptian people were also convinced of God's power. God can use judgment as well as forgiveness for the benefit of mankind.

The Hebrew Calendar

MONTH	TODAY'S CALENDAR	BIBLE REFERENCE	ISRAEL'S HOLIDAY
Nisan (Abib)	March - April	Exodus 13:4, 23:15, 34:18, Deuteronomy 16:1	Passover, Unleavened Bread, Firstfruits
Iyyar (Ziv)	April - May	1 Kings 6:1, 37	Second Passover
Sivan	May - June	Esther 8:9	Pentecost (Weeks)
Tammuz	June - July		
Ab	July - August		
Elul	August - September	Nehemiah 6:15	
Tishri (Ethanaim)	September - October	1 Kings 8:2	Trumpets, Day Of Atonement, Tabernacles (Booths)
Marcheshvan (Bul)	October - November	1 Kings 6:38	
Kislev	November - December	Nehemiah 1:1	Dedication (Hanukkah)
Tebeth	December - January	Esther 2:16	
Shebat	January - February	Zechariah 1:7	
Adar	February - March	Esther 3:7	Purim

Israel In The Desert

The Exodus
Exodus 12:31 – 12:42

Egypt had been severely plagued. The last one created a lot of deaths. One of those deaths was of Pharaoh's firstborn son. This incident brought him to his knees. He called for Moses and Aaron once again. This time, I think he was serious. He wanted them to take their people, including their herds and flocks, and leave Egypt. Pharaoh had full support from his fellow Egyptians. They wanted them gone, too.

Before the Israelites left, they took all of the bread dough they had made (without yeast) and wrapped it up for there travel. They also did as Moses instructed by asking the Egyptians for silver, gold and clothing. They freely gave them anything they wanted because God made this happen. Egypt basically got plundered by the Israelites and everyone was cool about it.

It has been estimated that the number of Israelites that left day was around two million people. They had been enslaved there for 430 years. They now had freedom and were no longer slaves. They traveled from Rameses to Succoth and baked cakes of unleavened bread from the dough they had brought with them. This was their first meal as a free people.

Passover Restrictions
Exodus 12:43 – 12:51

The Passover was a serious thing and had rules:

- No foreigner could eat of it.
- A slave that they bought could only eat as long as they were circumcised.
- Temporary residents and hired workers could not eat from it either.
- The meat had to be eaten inside one house. It was against the rules to eat it outside.
- They couldn't break any of the lamb's bones during the meat processing.
- It was to be celebrated as a community in Israel.
- If an alien (someone living in Israel, but wasn't born there) wanted to eat during the Passover, he would have to have all of the males in his home circumcised. The same law applied to both the alien and the person who was native of Israel.

The Israelites did as God commanded Moses and Aaron. This would be done every year for many generations to come.

Consecration Of The Firstborn
Exodus 13:1 – 13:16

God told Moses to consecrate to Him every firstborn male from the womb. This included humans and animals. Consecrate means to sacrifice or to consider something as belonging to God. This started another celebrated day that the Israelites commemorate called Firstfruits. This would be observed in the month of Abib (March – April). It would be a reminder that God delivered them from Egypt with his mighty hand.

According to God, they were not to eat nothing that contained yeast for seven days. On the seventh day, they were to hold a festival to God. This would be done every year and they would explain to their future generations what the event was all about and what it meant to Israel. It was important.

Crossing The Sea
Exodus 13:17 – 14:31

When Pharaoh let the people go, God didn't lead them on the short path through the Philistine country. If He did, the Israelites could have entered a war with them. Actually, the verses say they were prepared for battle when they left. Maybe the Philistine country was a hostile area. If you think about, how would you feel if you saw two million people coming to you at once? You would feel like this was an invasion. Instead, God sent them around the desert toward the Red Sea.

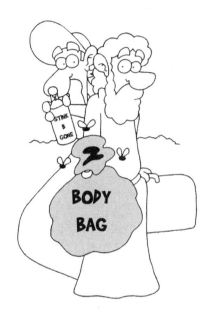

Moses brought along some stuff for his journey. The interesting thing to me is that he found some room in his luggage for some human remains. Yes, he was carrying someone's body parts. It was Joseph's bones. This was Moses' great uncle's bones from four generations back. What was he doing with them? It sounds creepy.

And Joseph took an oath of the children of Israel, saying, God will surely visit you, and ye shall carry up my bones from hence. So Joseph died, being an hundred and ten years old: and they embalmed him, and he was put in a coffin in Egypt. - Genesis 50: 25, 26

Moses was fulfilling an oath that Joseph had made with the sons of Israel. Joseph was part of his family tree. I thought that was cool.

God lead the Israelites on their journey. After they left Succoth, they camped at Etham at the edge of the desert. During the day, he appeared as a pillar of cloud. At night, he appeared as a pillar of fire. This made it possible for them to travel both day and night. He was always in the front leading them.

God told Moses to tell the Israelites to turn back. He wanted them to camp near Pi Hahiroth (which was between Migdol and the sea). They were to camp by the sea directly opposite of Baal Zephon. By doing so, Pharaoh would think the Israelites were lost and confused. After God hardened Pharaoh's heart, he and his army would try to pursue them. This would set Pharaoh up for another amazing miracle that both the Egyptians and the Israelites would see firsthand. So, the Israelites turned around.

Back in Egypt, Pharaoh was having second thoughts. Now that the Israelites were gone, they didn't have a labor force. There was no one to make the bricks. So, Pharaoh gathered his officers and chariots. They began a pursuit to get the Israelites back.

They met up with them at Pi Hahiroth and began marching towards them. The Israelites were freaking out. They immediately began regretting ever leaving Egypt. They didn't want to die out in the desert. They were stressing Moses out.

Moses tried comforting them by saying, "Don't be afraid. God will fight for us. Just stand still and watch His deliverance."

God spoke to Moses and told him to use his staff. When I first read it, it sounded like a scene from Star Wars where the green guy says, "Use the force...". God wanted Moses to stretch his staff over the sea to cause the waters to divide. After that, he and the Israelites could walk freely through the sea to the other side.

Unfortunately for the Egyptians, the divided waters would collapse on them as they followed behind. This was God's plan.

Moses did as God instructed by dividing the waters with his staff. The Israelites walked through the sea on dry ground with walls of water on both sides. The Egyptians tried following them on their chariots, but God caused their wheels to fall off. This slowed them down so that Moses and his people could continue without getting captured. As soon as they made it to the other side, Moses stretched out out his hand over the waters. This time the walls of water collapsed and engulfed the Egyptians and killed them. None of them survived.

As the Israelites looked back and saw all of the dead bodies that were on the shore, they realized that they just witnessed God's great power. From that point, they feared God and put their trust in Him and His servant, Moses.

I don't know about you, but walking through a sea of dry ground with walls of water on both sides would have been pretty scary. I guess it was better than standing there waiting for an angry Egyptian army to kill me. I would have at least brought a life jacket.

The Song Of Moses And Miriam

Exodus 15:1 – 15:21

Moses was royalty, a murderer, a husband, a father, a farmer, a servant of God, a leader of the Israelites and now... a poet and musician? He was one talented dude.

From these verses we get to read the lyrics of a song that Moses and the Israelites sang to God. Miriam (sister of Moses and Aaron) sang the last four lines while dancing with a tambourine. According to the verse, it seems that dancing can be used to praise God.

Here's a cool fact: It has been said that this Song Of Moses is the oldest recorded song in history. Pretty cool, huh?

Music was a big part of Israel's worship and celebration. Singing was an expression of love and thanks. It was also a great way of passing down oral traditions.

Music and singing is done in church today and has been part of a regular church service for several generations. The music played at the beginning of church services create a mood for worship and puts our hearts and our focus on God. It's a great way of praising Him.

The Waters Of Marah And Elim
Exodus 15:22 – 15:27

Moses led the Israelites from the Red Sea to the Desert of Shur. They had been traveling for 3 days without water. There was none to be found. When they reached Marah, they found water but it was too bitter to drink. The people started whining and complaining to Moses:

"What are we going to drink now?"

"Where's the 'good' water at?"

"You done got me out here with no water to drink. My throat's dry. I'm gonna die out here in the desert and it's gonna be your fault, Moses! You hearing me, Moses?!"

I'm sure poor Moses was stressed, so he cried out to God. God showed him a piece of wood that was laying around on the desert. Moses took the wood and threw it into the water at Marah. The bitter water became sweet.

God made a decree and a law for them that day and He tested them. He said, "If you listen carefully to My voice and do what is right in my eyes... If you pay attention to My commands and keep My decrees... I will not bring on you any of the diseases that I brought on the Egyptians. For I am God, the One that heals you."

At first, it sounds like God will severely punish the Israelites with diseases if they don't do exactly what He says. If a Israelite does something that goes against God, would he get zapped by God with a dose of gonorrhea?

I think God was telling them that by following His laws, it would protect them from harm. An example would be a law against prostitution that would keep them contracting venereal diseases. God's laws would be for their benefit as long as they followed them.

When they came to Elim, there were twelve springs and seventy palm trees. They camped there near the water.

Manna And Quail
Exodus 16:1 – 16:36

They left Elim and came to the Desert of Sin on the fifteenth day of the second month after they had came out of Egypt. This was between Elim and Sinai. In the desert, the Israelites started whining and complaining again to Moses and Aaron. This time they were hungry.

"We should of just died in Egypt! At least we had food. We had pots of meat and could eat all of the food we wanted. But you brought us out here in the desert to starve to death!"

God explained to Moses about He would be supplying them with food. For starters, bread would rain from heaven. The people would go out each day and gather enough for that day. On the sixth day, they are to gather a double portion. This would be enough for the sixth and seventh day.

Moses gave the Israelites the news that He received from God. God would be supplying their food. He would provide meat in the evening and bread in the morning every day except on the seventh. He also wanted them to realize where this food would be coming from – straight from God. He also cautioned them about all of the whining and complaining that they were doing. They weren't complaining to Moses, they were complaining against God. This wasn't a good thing.

Quail covered the camp that evening and in the morning there was a layer of dew around the camp. When the dew was gone, a thin layer of flakes appeared there on the desert ground. They Israelites didn't know what it was. Moses explained that it was bread that God had given them to eat. He reminded them to only take as much as they needed for the day – no more and no less.

Some of them didn't listen to Moses and took more than they needed. I guess they wanted to store it up for future use. Maybe they thought God wouldn't provide it the next day, so they kept some extra just in case. Or maybe some of them were greedy and just wanted more than everyone else. The problem with having more than a day's worth is that this extra bread would get infested with maggots and wouldn't be edible.

On the sixth day, the Israelites were instructed to gather twice as much bread as they would on any other day. On this day, they would prepare the extra bread for the following day because the seventh day would be a day of rest. This was called Sabbath Day.

This bread was called manna. It was white like a coriander seed and tasted like wafers made with honey. They ate this for forty years until they reached the border of Canaan.

God commanded Moses to save some of this manna for future generations to see. He kept about two quarts of it and placed it in a jar in front of the Testimony. Testimony?

The words 'testimony' and 'covenant' both refer to the conditional agreement made between God and the children of Israel at Mount Sinai.

And he gave unto Moses, when he had made an end of communing with him upon mount Sinai, two tables of testimony, tables of stone, written with the finger of God. - Exodus 31: 18

And Moses turned, and went down from the mount, and the two tables of the testimony were in his hand: the tables were written on both their sides; on the one side and on the other were they written. - Exodus 32: 15

Basically, I think Aaron placed the manna in front of the stone tablets that contained the Ten Commandments. Yes, the scene here is out of chronological order because God had given them the stone tablets yet. But, maybe it's mentioned so that we would know that this 'spot' would be the future home for it.

Water From The Rock
Exodus 17:1 – 17:7

The Israelites set out from the Desert of Sin. They went from place to place as God commanded. They camped at Rephidim and discovered that the place didn't have any drinking water. So, they started whining and complaining with Moses again. Moses got agitated. They were stressing him out and he didn't want them to make God mad, so he prayed about it.

"God, what am I supposed to do with these people? They are mad at me and they're getting on my last nerve!" Moses prayed.

God's answer was to take some elders and his staff in his hand. He wanted them to walk over to the rock at Horeb and strike it with the staff. By doing so, water would start coming out of it. This would be drinking water for the people. The elders saw the miracle and Moses named the place Massah and Meribah. This was because the Israelites basically 'scolded' Moses for their lack of water and because they tested God by asking, "Is God among us or not?"

The Amalekites Defeated
Exodus 17:8 – 17:16

The Amalekites attacked the Israelites in Rephidim. Joshua was Moses' military commander (second in command). Moses told him to take some of their men and fight the Amalekites. Moses would stand up on a hill with his staff in his hand.

Joseph battled the Amalekites just as Moses told him. Moses, Aaron and Hur stood on top of a hill. Moses had his staff in his hand. Every time Moses would raise the staff in the air, the

Israelites would start winning. But, when he would lower the staff, the Israelites would start losing. Every time Moses' arms got tired, he would have to take a break and lower them. It seems like Israel's victory depended upon Moses keeping his arms in the air.

I imaging Moses' arms was going numb by keeping them raised in the air for so long. Blood circulation may have decreased and cause his arms to fall asleep. He had to do something to keep that staff in the air. Aaron and Hur was there to help. They kept his arms raised up until sunset.

After their victory, God told Moses to write it down on a scroll so that Joshua could hear. God would erase the memory of Amalek from under heaven. Moses also built an altar and called it Jehovahnissi (The Lord Is My Banner).

For he said, Because the LORD hath sworn that the LORD will have war with Amalek from generation to generation. - Exodus 17: 16

Jethro Visits Moses
Exodus 18:1 – 18:27

Moses' father-inlaw, Jethro, had heard everything that God was doing for Moses and his people and how He had brought them out of Egypt. Moses had sent his wife, Zipporah, and their sons (Gershom and Eliezer) to stay with him. Jethro brought Moses' family to see him in the desert where he camped near the mountain of God. Moses met up with Jethro and did a lot of talking. Moses told him everything that God had been doing for the people of Israel. Moses, Aaron, Jethro and the elders basically praised God together for what He had done.

As Moses was setting up his seat as a judge of the people. Jethro couldn't help but notice that these people stood around him all day long doing nothing. Jethro questioned Moses about this.

"Something about this isn't right. What's going on here?" Jethro asked.

"Well, these people come to me to seek God's will. When they have problems, they come to me. I help them settle their differences, disputes and inform them of God's decrees and laws." Moses replied.

"This isn't good. These people are going to wear you out with all of their problems." Jethro said.

Keep in mind, we're talking about two million Israelites reporting to one man. That's a lot of drama for one person. I have a wife, four kids and two granddaughters. I can barely keep up with the drama that goes on in my house. I can't imagine what Moses was going through.

"The workload is too much for you. You're going to need some help. Here's what you can do. Set up some officials from the men that you consider trustworthy, honest and have a fear of God. Let them become judges of the people by handling smaller groups. If they have any major disputes and problems, they could bring those to you. This would lighten your load." Jethro said.

Moses did as Jethro said. He delegated the workload to his appointed officials. I think Moses needed to hear this from his father-inlaw. He may have been overloaded and didn't realize it. He may have just accepted 'stress' as part of the job. Now that he could share this stress with others, Moses could be more productive in doing the will of God.

Moses said his goodbyes and Jethro went back home to his country. This was a much needed visit.

Israel At Sinai

At Mount Sinai
Exodus 19:1 – 19:25

It was three months since they left Egypt. They were camping at the Desert of Sinai in front of the mountain – called Mount Sinai. Moses went up the mountain to talk with God. God gave him a message to tell the Israelites.

God had a purpose for rescuing the Israelites from slavery. He wanted to create a kingdom of priests and a holy nation. All they had to do was obey Him fully and keep His covenant. Although God owned the whole Earth, these people would be His 'chosen' ones.

Moses went back and gathered the elders. He prepared a speech to tell the Israelites about what God had told him. After he had spoken to the people, they were all in agreement to do whatever God wanted them to do. They were all on the same team. They would obey God and keep His covenant. Moses returned and told God the news.

God told Moses that He would come to him as a dense cloud. He would speak to Moses and He would do it in a way so that the Israelites could hear Him speaking. By doing so, the people would always put their trust in Moses. God also told Moses to go back to the people and consecrate them for two days. Consecrate? Consecrate would mean to prepare them for an upcoming holy occasion. It sounds like they had to wash their clothes. God was going to make a personal appearance at Mount Sinai on the third day.

God gave Moses a warning to tell the people about His upcoming appearance on Mount Sinai. The people had to keep their distance when He arrived. They couldn't climb up there to get a closer look. They couldn't even touch the mountain. If they did, they would die. They would have to wait to hear a long sounding blast from a ram's horn. After hearing this, the mountain would then be safe.

Moses climbed down the mountain. He consecrated the people and they washed their clothes. He told them to prepare themselves for the third day. And as added extra, he told them to abstain from sex for two days. This information may have created a sad moment for some of them. Washing their clothes may have made them a little uncomfortable, but... abstinence? I'm sure there were some emotions being expressed that day. Fortunately for them, it was for only two days.

On the morning of the third day, thunder and lightning filled the sky. A thick cloud covered the top of Mount Sinai as the Israelites heard a very loud trumpet blast. Hearing this made them tremble in fear. Moses led the people out of their camp and headed toward the foot of the mountain. Mount Sinai was covered in smoke because God ascended on it like fire. Smoke was coming out of the mountain like a furnace and the mountain shook. It may have been an earthquake. All the Israelites heard was the sound of a trumpet and it kept getting louder and louder.

Moses spoke and the voice of God answered him. God descended to the top of Mount Sinai and called Moses to come up. As soon as Moses made it to the top, God told him to go back down and warn the people to not try anything weird by climbing up to take a peak. God was serious because anyone that got too close would die. He did give one exception. Moses could bring his brother, Aaron, to join him.

The Ten Commandments
Exodus 20:1 – 20:21

This is where God gave Moses the Ten Commandments.

- *Thou shalt have no other gods before me.*
  - This can be anything that we put before God in our lives. It can be money, our jobs and just about anything we feel is more important than Him. It's about putting Him as number one on our priority list.
- *Thou shalt not make unto thee any graven image, or any likeness of any thing that is in heaven above, or that is in the earth beneath, or that is in the water under the earth:*

Thou shalt not bow down thyself to them, nor serve them: for I the LORD thy God am a jealous God, visiting the iniquity of the fathers upon the children unto the third and fourth generation of them that hate me; And shewing mercy unto thousands of them that love me, and keep my commandments.

- ○ This is about serving idols – images, statues and man-made things that we pray to and treat as a god.

- *Thou shalt not take the name of the LORD thy God in vain; for the LORD will not hold him guiltless that taketh his name in vain.*
  - ○ I grew up believing this meant to not use the name 'God' in cuss words. This is probably true. But, I've learned that it's more than that. It's when we say that we are children of God and we go around not acting like it in the way we conduct our lives from day to day.

- *Remember the sabbath day, to keep it holy. Six days shalt thou labour, and do all thy work: But the seventh day is the sabbath of the LORD thy God: in it thou shalt not do any work, thou, nor thy son, nor thy daughter, thy manservant, nor thy maidservant, nor thy cattle, nor thy stranger that is within thy gates: For in six days the LORD made heaven and earth, the sea, and all that in them is, and rested the seventh day: wherefore the LORD blessed the sabbath day, and hallowed it.*
  - ○ Basically, we work six days a week and rest on the seventh (Sabbath Day). But, what day is the Sabbath? For many of us, we think it's on Sunday. This is the day of the week that we sit in front of the TV and do absolutely nothing. Some of us attend church, go out to eat and come home and do absolutely nothing. The Hebrews back then, however, rested on Saturday.

- *Honour thy father and thy mother: that thy days may be long upon the land which the LORD thy God giveth thee.*

- This was a commandment that came with a reward for keeping it. If you honored your parents, you could live longer. If this rule applied today, many kids wouldn't live past their teenage years. But, this commandment was directed toward children. Kids should respect their parents.
- *Thou shalt not kill.*
  - Plain and simple. Don't kill. This commandment gets broken every day all over the world. Just turn on the news.
- *Thou shalt not commit adultery.*
  - If you're married, be true to your spouse. Don't go around cheating on them with another person. This would include fantasizing about it in our minds, too.
- *Thou shalt not steal.*
  - If it doesn't belong to you, leave it alone. It's not yours! Pretty simple.
- *Thou shalt not bear false witness against thy neighbour.*
  - Don't make up lies about other people. Don't create fake news. That would make you a liar. People that post on social media should probably take note.
- *Thou shalt not covet thy neighbour's house, thou shalt not covet thy neighbour's wife, nor his manservant, nor*

his maidservant, nor his ox, nor his ass, nor any thing that
is thy neighbour's. - Exodus 20: 3-17

- ○ Don't go around wanting what other people have. You
  don't have to keep up with the Jones'. Just take what
  you have and be thankful.

**Note: The Ten Commandments were directed toward the
people of Israel. The church today is under the New
Covenant, established by the death and resurrection of Jesus
Christ.**

The Israelites were blown away with fear as they stood their
distance watching and hearing everything that was going on up
there on that mountain. Even the voice of God was freaking them
out. They asked Moses if he could tell God to tone it down a bit.
They only wanted to hear from Moses and not God because His
voice made them scared. Moses assured them that this was how
God intended it to be. He wanted them to fear Him and to always
remember this fear for Him. It would keep them from sinning.

Idols And Altars
Exodus 20:22 – 20:26

Even though the Israelites had seen and heard God speak to
Moses on the mountain, He knew that one day they would start
worshiping idols. He knew the future and probably saw these
people creating statues and little trinkets of gold and silver. They
would give them names and start treating them as gods. God
warned them ahead of time. We will read later in the Old
Testament books that they eventually did.

I guess as time go on, people easily forget. All that the Israelites saw and heard of God personally became stories that they told their future generations. These stories may have sounded like fables over time. These people may have wanted a god that they could see and disregarded God that their ancestors had told them about. But, in these verses, God knew that it would happen.

God wanted His people to build altars to Him and make animal sacrifices. He was very specific on how He wanted these altars to look. He wanted them earthy and not man-made out of some type of synthetic plastics or re-purposed items like they do on Pinterest. He didn't even want the altars to have steps. Why? The verses say that it would show their nakedness. How? The only thing that comes to mind is that underwear wasn't invented yet. The higher a person goes up, the more a person standing below can see. 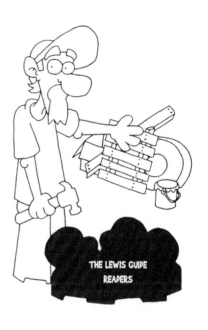 Know what I'm saying? That's why women today shouldn't climb ladders with dresses on. Nobody wants to see all that.

Hebrew Servants
Exodus 21:1 – 21:11

Beginning in Chapter 19, God was giving laws to Moses to share with the people of Israel. They were to follow them. God was creating a nation of His chosen people. These laws were for their benefit.

These verses are concerning Hebrew servants and how to properly treat them. These were God's chosen people, too. The Hebrews were freed from slavery when they left Egypt, but they may have become slaves again due to poverty, debt or even crime. But, God wanted them to be treated as humans and not property. They were allowed to work their way to freedom.

A person could own a slave for six years. After that, they had to let them go free. If the slave had a wife, both would have to be set free. If the master gave them a wife and she had kids, the woman and her kids belonged to the master. The man slave could go free. If, by chance, the man slave wanted to stay a slave to his master, the master would have to take him to the judges and have his ear pierced. Then he would be his servant for life.

If a man sells his daughter as a servant, she is not allowed to be set free. If the master was unsatisfied with her, he must let her be redeemed. If he selects her for his son, he must grant her rights of a daughter. If the son marries another woman, he must not deprive the first one of her food, clothing and marital rights. If he does not provide her with these three things, she is free to go without payment or money.

Personal Injuries
Exodus 21:12 – 21:36

These are laws that God gave that pertain to personal injury:

- If anyone strikes and kills a man, they are to be put to death. If it was by accident (meaning God allowed it to happen), the person must flee to a place that God would designate. The common penalty for first degree murder in the USA today is life in prison. On some occasions a murderer is executed.
- Anyone that attacks his father or his mother must be put to death.
- Anyone that kidnaps another and either sells them or is caught with them must be put to death. In the USA today, a kidnapper can be imprisoned up to 20 years or more and fined up to $50,000.
- Anyone who curses his father or mother must be put to death. I imagine the kids back in the day respected their parents.
- If two men are fighting and one hits the other with a stone or his fists and it causes him to be confined to a bed, the one that hit him must pay for the time he lost and see that he is healed. If this applied today, a normal bar room brawl could result in the 'winner' paying the 'losers' bills for a while.
- If a man beats his male or female slave with a rod, and the slave dies, the man must be punished. If the slave does not die and gets back up after a day or two, the man does not get punished because the slave is his property.
- If men are fighting, and a pregnant woman gets hit in the process, there are two verdicts. If the woman gives birth prematurely but has no serious injury, the person that hit

her must pay whatever her husband demands and what the court allows. If there is serious injury, the court will rule life for a life, eye for an eye, tooth for tooth, hand for hand, foot for foot, burn for burn, wound for wound and bruise for bruise. Basically whatever happens to the woman will happen to them.

- If a man hits his manservant or maidservant in the eye and it destroys it, he must let them go free. If he knocks out their tooth, he must let them go free.

- If a bull gores and kills a man or woman, the bull will be stoned to death and it's meat must not be eaten. It's owner will not be held responsible. If the bull has a record of goring people and it's owner has been made aware of this problem and it kills someone, both the bull and it's owner will be put to death. The owner could redeem his life if payment is demanded instead. He will have to pay whatever is asked. If the bull gores a male or female slave, the bull will be stoned to death and it's owner will be fined thirty shekels to the master of the slave. I read that thirty shekels back in those days was the equivalent of about 4 months worth of pay.

- If an ox or donkey falls in a hole that someone dug up and fails to cover it, this person will pay the animal's owner for the loss. He will also own the dead animal.

78

- If a man's bull injures the bull of anther and it dies, they are to sell both bulls and divide the money. If the bull does this on a regular basis and the owner is negligent about pinning him up, he must sell his bull and give this money to the owner of the dead bull and can keep the dead bull.

Protection Of Property
Exodus 22:1 – 22:15

These are laws that God gave concerning protecting people's property:

- If a man steals an ox or a sheep and sells it or slaughters it, he must repay the owner five heads of cattle for the ox or four sheep for the sheep. In Georgia today, a thief that stole something (that was valued at $500 or less) would be fined no more than $1000 and would be sent to jail for no longer than twelve months. The person he stole from would have to sue the thief to get his property value back and will have to pay the court costs to do it. In most cases, a thief will not have the money to pay, which makes suing them useless. Who really benefits? The court system.
- If a thief is caught breaking in and gets killed by the one protecting themselves and their belongings, the defender is not guilty of murder. If it happens after sunrise, the defender is considered guilty. I guess it was better to let a thief steal from you than to kill him. If the thief is caught, he would have to pay the person back. If he was broke, he would be sold as a slave and work until his debt was paid. If the thief stole an animal, he would have to pay back double.

79

- If a man's livestock wanders off into someone else field or vineyard, he must make restitution by replacing what his animals ate or destroyed from the best of his own field or vineyard.
- If a fire breaks out and it destroys someone's field, the person that started the fire must make restitution.
- If a man gives his neighbor silver or goods for safekeeping and they become stolen, the thief (if caught) must pay back double. If the thief is not found, the owner of the house must appear before the judges to determine whether he had anything to do with the crime. In all cases of illegal possession of personal property, both parties involved will have to appear before the judges to determine who is guilty or innocent. The guilty party will have to pay back double.
- If a man gives an animal to his neighbor for safekeeping and it dies or gets injured or becomes stolen, the issue will be settled by taking an oath before God. The owner is to accept this and no restitution would be required. If the animal was stolen from the neighbor, he must make restitution to the owner. If the animal died because he was ripped apart by another animal, the neighbor is to bring those icky pieces as evidence and he will not be required to pay for the torn animal.
- If a man borrows an animal from his neighbor and it becomes injured or it dies and the owner is not present, he must make restitution. If the owner is with the animal, the borrower will not have to pay. If the animal was hired, the money paid for the hire covers the loss.

Social Responsibility
Exodus 22:16 – 22:31

Being an Israelite meant you had social responsibilities that God made into a law:

- If a man seduces a virgin, who is not pledged to be married, and sleeps with her, he must pay the bride-price and she shall be his wife. If her father refuses to give her to him, he must still pay the bride-price for virgins. I would assume the 'bride-price' was set by the girl's father.
- Do not allow a sorceress to live. These were people that summoned demons, cast spells and did a lot of strange magic. God was totally against this. The Harry Potter series would not have been popular back in those days.

- Anyone that has sex with an animal must die. Maybe this was a problem back then? I really don't want to know.
- Anyone that sacrifices to any god other than the Lord must be destroyed.
- Do not mistreat or oppress anyone that comes from another country.
- Do not take advantage of a widow or an orphan. God would kill you

and make your wives become widows and your children would become fatherless.

- If you lend money to an Israelite, do not charge them interest. If you use his cloak as collateral for the loan, give it back to him by sunset. Imagine a loan without interest. That would be nice, wouldn't it?
- Do not blaspheme God.
- Do not hold back offerings from your granaries or vats.
- You must give God the firstborn of your sons. Do the same with your cattle and your sheep. Let them stay with their mothers for seven days and give them to God on the eighth.
- Do not eat the meat of animals torn by wild beasts.

Laws Of Justice And Mercy
Exodus 23:1 – 23:9

These are the laws that God gave them about justice and mercy:

- Do not go around telling things that aren't true about someone. Don't help a wicked person by being a false witness. Fake news was definitely prohibited. Nowadays, it's just part of the social newsfeed.
- Just because a 'crowd' is doing some wrong, doesn't mean you have to follow them. When you give a testimony in court, don't side with the crowd. For example, if the crowd says someone is guilty (but you know he's innocent), don't say he's guilty just because the crowd said it. And just because a person is poor, don't show him favoritism in a lawsuit situation.
- If you see someone's wandering animal, take it back to them. If you see a person (that hates you) having some difficulty with their animal, help them with it.

- Do not deny justice to the poor in their lawsuits. Have nothing to do with false charges. Do not put an innocent or honest person to death.
- Do not accept a bribe because It will blind those that see and will twist the words of the righteous.
- Do not oppress an 'alien'. This was mentioned twice so far in two law categories. This was important. God reminded them of how it felt to be an 'alien' in Egypt, so they shouldn't treat others this way.

Sabbath Laws
Exodus 23:10 – 23:13

The were the laws about Sabbath that God gave them:

- For six years, a person could work their land growing and harvesting crops. But, on the seventh year, they are not to use it and just let it grow up. Whatever grows could be eaten by the poor and the wild animals.
- For six days, a person could work. They were to rest on the seventh day. This law applied to their livestock and people that worked for them. This would give everyone a day to rest.

God told them to be careful and observe all of the laws that He gave. In addition, they are not to even speak the names of other gods.

The Three Annual Festivals
Exodus 23:14 – 23:19

There were three festivals that God wanted them to celebrate to Him:

1. **Feast Of Unleavened Bread**
   - ○ For seven days, they were to eat bread made without yeast. This would be done in the month of Abib to celebrate the month that they left Egypt.
2. **Feast Of Harvesting**
   - ○ They were to celebrate with the firstfruits of the crops they sowed in their fields.
3. **Feast Of Ingathering**
   - ○ This was to be celebrated at the end of the year when they gathered in their crops from the field.

These festivals had special instructions:

- Three times per year, the people were to gather before God.
- Their sacrifices should not contain any yeast.
- The fat of any offerings to God should not be kept until morning. The firstfruits that the people brought should be their very best from their fields.
- They were told not to cook a young goat in its mother's milk.

God's Angel To Prepare The Way
Exodus 23:20 – 23:33

It was time for Moses and the Israelites to move on. God would be sending them to the land of the Amorites, Hittites, Perizzites, Canaanites, Hivites and Jebusites. God had already sent an angel ahead of them to prepare the way. This angel would guard them against anyone that wanted to oppose them on their journey. All Moses had to do was pay attention to him and listen to what he had to say. Undoubtedly, they were heading towards hostile territory. If they acted in their own strength or chose to ignore

God's instructions, they could have died. But God would be acting on Moses' behalf by wiping these enemies off the land.

This would be the land that Moses and the Israelites would possess. But first, the current owners had to be removed. God would take care of this over time. He wanted to make sure the Israelites didn't arrive and start worshiping their idols and following along with their pagan activities. Instead, He wanted them to destroy them and their sacred stones. By worshiping only God, He would bless them with sufficient food and water, good health, plenty of offspring and a full life span.

The Covenant Confirmed
Exodus 24:1 – 24:18

God called a meeting with Moses, Aaron, Nadab, Abihu and seventy of the elders of Israel at the top of Mount Sinai. Out of all of these people, only Moses could talk to God face-to-face. Everyone else had to keep their distance. Before they could start their meeting, Moses set up an altar and twelve pillars at the foot of the mountain. He performed a ceremony that involved burnt offerings and the blood of young bulls.

The seventy-four men went up the mountain to meet with God. From a distance they saw God. Under Him was pavement of sapphire and it was clear as the sky. God instructed Moses to continue climbing to the top of the mountain to where He was. God was going to give him the stone tablets that contained the law and commands that God would write for the Israelites.

As Moses reached the top of the mountain, all you could see was clouds. It sounds like the verses tells us that Moses stayed up there in those clouds for six days before God called out to him on the seventh. When He spoke, the Israelites (from below) saw a consuming fire. Moses entered the clouds and stayed there on that mountain for forty days and forty nights.

Offerings For The Tabernacle
Exodus 25:1 – 25:9

God told Moses to tell the people of Israel to make him an offering, but only from the ones who felt it in their hearts to do so. These would be things they should offer to God:

- Gold, silver and bronze
- Blue, purple and scarlet yarn and fine linen
- Goat hair
- Ram skins (dyed red)
- Hides of sea cows
- Acacia wood
- Olive oil
- Spices
- Onyx stones and other gems

Many of these things carry a large price tag. You start talking about offering precious metals and gems, you're talking about money. Back in those days, things weren't ordered online and imported from China for pennies on the dollar. This was expensive stuff and some of it was probably hard to get. I'm sure there were many debates among the families about if they should they part with it or not. I mean, giving goat hair might not have been a big deal, but parting with gold or a cup of cinnamon spice might have been debated upon.

God also told him to have his people build him a tabernacle. This tabernacle would be built by the Israelites as a sanctuary for God and He would dwell among them. It and its furnishings had to be made to His specs. They couldn't just throw something together from scrap wood laying around in their garage. This was special.

The Ark
Exodus 25:10 – 25:22

Cool facts about the ark:

- This was a chest made from acacia wood. Acacia wood was a common wood that was easily available back in those days. Unlike pine, acacia wood is very durable and strong. Things made from it would last a very long time.

- It was 2.5 cubits x 1.5 cubits x 1.5 cubits (1 cubit = 1.5 feet. So, basically, 3.75 feet x 2.25 feet x 2.25 feet).
- It had to be overlayed with gold (inside and out) with gold molding around it.
- It had four gold rings fastened to its feet.
- It had two rings attached to both sides of this chest. Two poles, made from acacia wood and overlayed in gold, was attached through the two rings on the side of the chest. These poles would never be removed.
- Inside this chest, Moses would place the Testimony that God was about to give him.

Here again, this was special and had to be made to spec. This couldn't be made from particle board and a few Philips head screws. God was specific.

The Table
Exodus 25:23 – 25:30

God wanted Moses to build a table. He couldn't just buy one on sale at Ashley Furniture. He wanted something built from scratch and not something made from plywood from the local Home Depot. Not only did he have to build the table, he had to make the dishes, pitchers and bowls. He had specs:

- The table would be made of acacia wood.
- The size would be two cubits long, a cubit wide and a cubit and a half high (roughly 3 feet x 1.5 feet x 9 inches). It sounds kind of small for a table.
- It would be overlayed with pure gold and with gold molding around it.

- It would have a rim with gold around it.
- It would have four gold rings for the table and it would be fastened to the four corners, where the four legs are.
- The rings were to be close to the rim to hold the poles used in carrying the table.
- He would make poles of acacia wood, overlay them with gold, and would carry the table with them.
- The plates and dishes would be made of pure gold, as well as its pitchers and bowls for the pouring out of offerings.
- The bread of the Presence would be placed on this table to be presented to God at all times.

The Lampstand
Exodus 25:31 – 25:40

Gold told Moses to build a lampstand. A lamp stand? In my mind, this is something that looks like a metal pole that sits on heavy metal base that has light fixtures on it (usually about 3 lights). You can get these at Walmart for about $15. It does require assembly, but it's pretty easy to do. You don't even have to read the instructions. Unfortunately, this isn't what God had in mind. As usual, God had specs to follow:

- He was to make a lampstand of pure gold - hammered out on its base and shaft and the flowerlike cups, buds and blossoms would be made out of one piece.
- Six branches were to extend from the sides of the lampstand - three on one side and three on the other.
- Three cups shaped like almond flowers with buds and blossoms were to be on one branch, three on the next branch, and the same for all six branches extending from the lampstand.

- And on the lampstand there were to be four cups shaped like almond flowers with buds and blossoms.
- One bud should be under the first pair of branches extending from the lampstand, a second bud under the second pair, and a third bud under the third pair—six branches in all.
- The buds and branches should all be of one piece with the lampstand, hammered out of pure gold.
- He would make its seven lamps and set them up on it so that they light the space in front of it.
- The wick trimmers and trays are to be of pure gold.
- A talent of pure gold would be used for the lampstand and all these accessories. Some say a talent weighs about 33 kilograms. As of 2018, this would be worth 1.4 million dollars. This was a serious lamp stand.
- It was important that Moses built this to spec (according to God).

The Tabernacle
Exodus 26:1 – 26:37

This tabernacle was a portable sanctuary that God instructed Moses to build. It would be the place of worship for the Hebrew tribes. They would travel with this thing until they reached the Promised Land. It appears to have been made of wood and a bunch of curtains. It wasn't made from wavy 2x4's from your local lumber yard and curtains you would get second-handed from a thrift store. God was specific about this. This is what He told Moses:

- Make the tabernacle with ten curtains of finely twisted linen and blue, purple and scarlet yarn, with cherubim woven into them by a skilled worker. Not just anyone could make these curtains!

- All the curtains are to be the same size—twenty-eight cubits long and four cubits wide. A cubit is about 1.5 feet. These curtains would be 42 feet long and 6 feet wide. These were serious curtains.
- Join five of the curtains together, and do the same with the other five.
- Make loops of blue material along the edge of the end curtain in one set, and do the same with the end curtain in the other set.
- Make fifty loops on one curtain and fifty loops on the end curtain of the other set, with the loops opposite each other.
- Then make fifty gold clasps and use them to fasten the curtains together so that the tabernacle is a unit.
- Make curtains of goat hair for the tent over the tabernacle—eleven altogether.
- All eleven curtains are to be the same size—thirty cubits long and four cubits wide. We're taking 45 feet long by 6 feet wide.
- Join five of the curtains together into one set and the other six into another set. Fold the sixth curtain double at the front of the tent.
- Make fifty loops along the edge of the end curtain in one set and also along the edge of the end curtain in the other set.
- Then make fifty bronze clasps and put them in the loops to fasten the tent together as a unit.
- As for the additional length of the tent curtains, the half curtain that is left over is to hang down at the rear of the tabernacle.

- The tent curtains will be a cubit longer (or 1.5 feet) on both sides; what is left will hang over the sides of the tabernacle so as to cover it.
- Make for the tent a covering of ram skins dyed red, and over that a covering of the other durable leather. Durable leather? Full grain leather is what we currently consider the best leather. It has not been snuffed, sanded, or buffed to remove any natural marks or imperfections from its surface. Its fibers are stable and durable because the grain has not been removed. Aniline leather is the most desirable finish in the manufacture of leather.
- Make upright frames of acacia wood for the tabernacle.
- Each frame is to be ten cubits long and a cubit and a half wide, (this would be 15 feet long by 2.25 feet wide) with two projections set parallel to each other. Make all the frames of the tabernacle in this way.
- Make twenty frames for the south side of the tabernacle and make forty silver bases to go under them—two bases for each frame, one under each projection.
- For the other side, the north side of the tabernacle, make twenty frames and forty silver bases—two under each frame.
- Make six frames for the far end, that is, the west end of the tabernacle, and make two frames for the corners at the far end. At these two corners they must be double from the bottom all the way to the top and fitted into a single ring; both shall be like that. So there will be eight frames and sixteen silver bases—two under each frame.
- Also make crossbars of acacia wood: five for the frames on one side of the tabernacle, five for those on the other side, and five for the frames on the west, at the far end of the tabernacle.

- The center crossbar is to extend from end to end at the middle of the frames.
- Overlay the frames with gold and make gold rings to hold the crossbars. Also overlay the crossbars with gold.
- Make a curtain of blue, purple and scarlet yarn and finely twisted linen, with cherubim woven into it by a skilled worker.
- Hang it with gold hooks on four posts of acacia wood overlaid with gold and standing on four silver bases.
- Hang the curtain from the clasps and place the ark of the covenant law behind the curtain. The curtain will separate the Holy Place from the Most Holy Place.
- Put the atonement cover on the ark of the covenant law in the Most Holy Place.
- Place the table outside the curtain on the north side of the tabernacle and put the lampstand opposite it on the south side.
- For the entrance to the tent make a curtain of blue, purple and scarlet yarn and finely twisted linen—the work of an embroiderer.
- Make gold hooks for this curtain and five posts of acacia wood overlaid with gold. And cast five bronze bases for them.

To be a portable sanctuary, this thing was huge. I imagine it took several people to carry it around. They took it everywhere they went.

The Altar Of Burnt Offering
Exodus 27:1 – 27:8

Now Moses is building an altar for burnt offerings. He couldn't just rake an area on the ground, throw some dead tree limbs around and burn stuff. God was specific. Here's what He wanted him to build:

- Build an altar of acacia wood, three cubit high (roughly 4.5 feet high); it is to be square, five cubits long and five cubits wide (7.5 feet by 7.5 feet).
- Make a horn at each of the four corners, so that the horns and the altar are of one piece, and overlay the altar with bronze.
- Make all its utensils of bronze—its pots to remove the ashes, and its shovels, sprinkling bowls, meat forks and firepans.
- Make a grating for it, a bronze network, and make a bronze ring at each of the four corners of the network.
- Put it under the ledge of the altar so that it is halfway up the altar.
- Make poles of acacia wood for the altar and overlay them with bronze.
- The poles are to be inserted into the rings so they will be on two sides of the altar when it is carried.

- Make the altar hollow, out of boards.

God told Moses how to make this thing on the mountain, along with all the other stuff He wanted him to build. Moses had to have taken plenty of notes. This is a lot of stuff to build and God was serious about the measurements, materials and who He wanted to actually build it. He wanted skilled people.

The Courtyard
Exodus 27:9 – 27:19

As Moses and the Hebrew people journeyed across the land, they had to make sure they had plenty of room to set up their tabernacle. They couldn't just put it anywhere. God was specific about this, too. Here are His specs:

- Make a courtyard for the tabernacle. The south side shall be a hundred cubits (150 feet) long and is to have curtains of finely twisted linen, with twenty posts and twenty bronze bases and with silver hooks and bands on the posts.
- The north side shall also be a hundred cubits (150 feet) long and is to have curtains, with twenty posts and twenty bronze bases and with silver hooks and bands on the posts.
- The west end of the courtyard shall be fifty cubits (75 feet) wide and have curtains, with ten posts and ten bases.
- On the east end, toward the sunrise, the courtyard shall also be fifty cubits (75 feet) wide.
- Curtains fifteen cubits (22.5 feet) long are to be on one side of the entrance, with three posts and three bases,

and curtains fifteen cubits (22.5 feet) long are to be on the other side, with three posts and three bases.

- For the entrance to the courtyard, provide a curtain twenty cubits (30 feet) long, of blue, purple and scarlet yarn and finely twisted linen—the work of an embroiderer—with four posts and four bases.
- All the posts around the courtyard are to have silver bands and hooks, and bronze bases.
- The courtyard shall be a hundred cubits (150 feet) long and fifty cubits (75 feet) wide, with curtains of finely twisted linen five cubits(7.5 feet) high, and with bronze bases.
- All the other articles used in the service of the tabernacle, whatever their function, including all the tent pegs for it and those for the courtyard, are to be of bronze.

Interesting thing to me is that the things made for inside the tent was made from gold and everything made outside of the tent was made of bronze. There may be a purpose or symbolism behind that.

Oil For The Lampstand
Exodus 27:20 – 27:21

God tells Moses to tell the
Israelites to bring him some oil for
the lamps so that they would stay
burning. But, not just any oil. Oh,
no! This would be oil from
pressed olives. It sounds to me
like the same olives you would
put in a fancy salad can also be
used to produce fuel for an oil
lamp. We may want to reconsider
it as a salad-topper. Or, for safety
reasons, we may want to stay far
away from open fires during the
digestive process. It's better to be
safe than sorry. Know what I
mean?

Aaron and his sons get the job of keeping the lamps burning from
morning until nighttime. This would be performed in the tent of
meeting, outside the curtain that shields the ark of the covenant
law. This would be the rule among the Israelites for the
generations to come. That's a lot of olives!

The Priestly Garments
Exodus 28:1 – 28:5

God wanted Aaron (Moses' brother) and his sons (Nadab, Abihu,
Eleazar and Ithama) to be His priests. He also wanted Moses to
make the garments that they would wear as priests to give them
dignity and honor. Moses had to look around for some skilled
workers to do this difficult task. God wanted sacred garments:

a breastpiece
an ephod
a robe
a woven tunic
a turban
a sash

They were to be made from gold, yarn and fine linen (preferably blue, purple and scarlet). Nothing red, pink or pastel puke brown!

The Ephod
Exodus 28:6 – 28:14

What is an ephod? I personally don't have a clue. It's not a word I use every day. However, it

does sound like a name for a cute fish for an aquarium. But, it's not. The dictionary says an ephod is a sleeveless garment worn by Jewish priests. I would have never known.

God wanted to make sure that His priests looked good. He put a lot of details into it that He wanted Moses to make happen. Here's how He wanted Moses to make an ephod to look like:

- Make the ephod of gold, and of blue, purple and

scarlet yarn, and of finely twisted linen—the work of skilled hands. Not just anyone could sew up an ephod!

- It is to have two shoulder pieces attached to two of its corners, so it can be fastened.
- Its skillfully woven waistband is to be like it—of one piece with the ephod and made with gold, and with blue, purple and scarlet yarn, and with finely twisted linen.
- Take two onyx stones and engrave on them the names of the sons of Israel in the order of their birth—six names on one stone and the remaining six on the other.
- Engrave the names of the sons of Israel on the two stones the way a gem cutter engraves a seal. Then mount the stones in gold filigree settings and fasten them on the shoulder pieces of the ephod as memorial stones for the sons of Israel. Aaron is to bear the names on his shoulders as a memorial before the Lord.
- Make gold filigree settings and two braided chains of pure gold, like a rope, and attach the chains to the settings.

I imagine the priests back in the day looked fairly spiffy with their super cool looking ephods. It was by God's design. Just sayin'.

The Breastpiece
Exodus 28:15 – 28:30

The main purpose of the High Priest's breastplate was to be a memorial (reminder) before God. It was meant to remind him that he represented all the people, as mediator and intercessor, before the Lord. The person that wore this knew they had a big responsibility. Here's what God told Moses about how He wanted them made:

- Fashion a breastpiece for making decisions— the work of skilled hands. Make it like the ephod: of gold, and of blue, purple and scarlet yarn, and of finely twisted linen.
- It is to be square - a span long and a span wide - and folded double. (According to what I've read, a span is roughly 9 inches.)
- Then mount four rows of precious stones on it. The first row shall be carnelian, chrysolite and beryl; the second row shall be turquoise, lapis lazuli and emerald; the third row shall be jacinth, agate and amethyst; the fourth row shall be topaz, onyx and jasper. Mount them in gold filigree settings.
- There are to be twelve stones, one for each of the names of the sons of Israel, each engraved like a seal with the name of one of the twelve tribes.

- For the breastpiece make braided chains of pure gold, like a rope.
- Make two gold rings for it and fasten them to two corners of the breastpiece.
- Fasten the two gold chains to the rings at the corners of the breastpiece, and the other ends of the chains to the two settings, attaching them to the shoulder pieces of the ephod at the front.
- Make two gold rings and attach them to the other two corners of the breastpiece on the inside edge next to the ephod.
- Make two more gold rings and attach them to the bottom of the shoulder pieces on the front of the ephod, close to the seam just above the waistband of the ephod.
- The rings of the breastpiece are to be tied to the rings of the ephod with blue cord, connecting it to the waistband, so that the breastpiece will not swing out from the ephod.
- Whenever Aaron enters the Holy Place, he will bear the names of the sons of Israel over his heart on the breastpiece of decision as a continuing memorial before the Lord.
- Also put the Urim and the Thummim in the breastpiece, so they may be over Aaron's heart whenever he enters the presence of the LORD. Thus Aaron will always bear the means of making decisions for the Israelites over his heart before the Lord.

Other Priestly Garments
Exodus 28:31 – 28:43

The priests were undoubtedly very important people in the sight of God. He must have held them up to high standards in the way they acted and dressed. Here are more of His instructions to Moses on how to properly dress them and how to treat them as they performed the duties God had for them to do:

- Make the robe of the ephod entirely of blue cloth, with an opening for the head in its center. There shall be a woven edge like a collar around this opening, so that it will not tear.

- Make pomegranates of blue, purple and scarlet yarn around the hem of the robe, with gold bells between them. The gold bells and the pomegranates are to alternate around the hem of the robe.

- Aaron must wear it when he ministers. The sound of the bells will be heard when he enters the Holy Place before the Lord and when he comes out, so that he will not die.

- Make a plate of pure gold and engrave on it as on a seal: holy to the Lord.

- Fasten a blue cord to it to attach it to the turban; it is to be on the front of the turban. It will be on Aaron's forehead, and he will bear the guilt involved in the sacred gifts the Israelites consecrate, whatever their gifts may be. It will be on Aaron's forehead continually so that they will be acceptable to the Lord.

- Weave the tunic of fine linen and make the turban of fine linen. The sash is to be the work of an embroiderer.
- Make tunics, sashes and caps for Aaron's sons to give them dignity and honor.
- After you put these clothes on your brother Aaron and his sons, anoint and ordain them. Consecrate them so they may serve me as priests.
- Make linen undergarments as a covering for the body, reaching from the waist to the thigh.
- Aaron and his sons must wear them whenever they enter the tent of meeting or approach the altar to minister in the Holy Place, so that they will not incur guilt and die. This is to be a lasting ordinance for Aaron and his descendants.

Consecration Of The Priests
Exodus 29:1 – 29:46

Consecrate means to make holy or to dedicate to a higher purpose. Back in the day, there were things that had to happen before someone could perform the duties of a priest. A person couldn't just wake up one morning and say, "You know what? Today I will be a priest. I will do all the things that priests do. Starting now." That's not how it worked.

103

Here's how God wanted Moses to consecrate His priests:

- Take a young bull and two rams without defect.
- And from the finest wheat flour make round loaves without yeast, thick loaves without yeast and with olive oil mixed in, and thin loaves without yeast and brushed with olive oil.
- Put them in a basket and present them along with the bull and the two rams.
- Then bring Aaron and his sons to the entrance to the tent of meeting and wash them with water.
- Take the garments and dress Aaron with the tunic, the robe of the ephod, the ephod itself and the breastpiece. Fasten the ephod on him by its skillfully woven waistband.
- Put the turban on his head and attach the sacred emblem to the turban.
- Take the anointing oil and anoint him by pouring it on his head.
- Bring his sons and dress them in tunics
- and fasten caps on them. Then tie sashes on Aaron and his sons. The priesthood is theirs by a lasting ordinance. "Then you shall ordain Aaron and his sons.
- Bring the bull to the front of the tent of meeting, and Aaron and his sons shall lay their hands on its head.
- Slaughter it in the Lord's presence at the entrance to the tent of meeting.
- Take some of the bull's blood and put it on the horns of the altar with your finger, and pour out the rest of it at the base of the altar.
- Then take all the fat on the internal organs, the long lobe of the liver, and both kidneys with the fat on them, and burn them on the altar.

- But burn the bull's flesh and its hide and its intestines outside the camp. It is a sin offering.
- Take one of the rams, and Aaron and his sons shall lay their hands on its head.
- Slaughter it and take the blood and splash it against the sides of the altar.
- Cut the ram into pieces and wash the internal organs and the legs, putting them with the head and the other pieces.
- Then burn the entire ram on the altar. It is a burnt offering to the Lord, a pleasing aroma, a food offering presented to the Lord.
- Take the other ram, and Aaron and his sons shall lay their hands on its head.
- Slaughter it, take some of its blood and put it on the lobes of the right ears of Aaron and his sons, on the thumbs of their right hands, and on the big toes of their right feet. Then splash blood against the sides of the altar.
- And take some blood from the altar and some of the anointing oil and sprinkle it on Aaron and his garments and on his sons and their garments. Then he and his sons and their garments will be consecrated.
- Take from this ram the fat, the fat tail, the fat on the internal organs, the long lobe of the liver, both kidneys with the fat on them, and the right thigh. (This is the ram for the ordination.)
- From the basket of bread made without yeast, which is before the Lord, take one round loaf, one thick loaf with olive oil mixed in, and one thin loaf.
- Put all these in the hands of Aaron and his sons and have them wave them before the Lord as a wave offering.

- Then take them from their hands and burn them on the altar along with the burnt offering for a pleasing aroma to the Lord, a food offering presented to the Lord.
- After you take the breast of the ram for Aaron's ordination, wave it before the Lord as a wave offering, and it will be your share.
- Consecrate those parts of the ordination ram that belong to Aaron and his sons: the breast that was waved and the thigh that was presented.
- This is always to be the perpetual share from the Israelites for Aaron and his sons. It is the contribution the Israelites are to make to the Lord from their fellowship offerings.
- Aaron's sacred garments will belong to his descendants so that they can be anointed and ordained in them.
- The son who succeeds him as priest and comes to the tent of meeting to minister in the Holy Place is to wear them seven days.
- Take the ram for the ordination and cook the meat in a sacred place.
- At the entrance to the tent of meeting, Aaron and his sons are to eat the meat of the ram and the bread that is in the basket.
- They are to eat these offerings by which atonement was made for their ordination and consecration. But no one else may eat them, because they are sacred.
- And if any of the meat of the ordination ram or any bread is left over till morning, burn it up. It must not be eaten, because it is sacred.
- Do for Aaron and his sons everything I have commanded you, taking seven days to ordain them.

- Sacrifice a bull each day as a sin offering to make atonement. Purify the altar by making atonement for it, and anoint it to consecrate it.
- For seven days make atonement for the altar and consecrate it. Then the altar will be most holy, and whatever touches it will be holy.
- This is what you are to offer on the altar regularly each day: two lambs a year old. Offer one in the morning and the other at twilight.
- With the first lamb offer a tenth of an ephah (roughly 15 cups) of the finest flour mixed with a quarter of a hin (a little over 5 cups) of oil from pressed olives, and a quarter of a hin (a little over 5 cups) of wine as a drink offering.
- Sacrifice the other lamb at twilight with the same grain offering and its drink offering as in the morning—a pleasing aroma, a food offering presented to the Lord.
- For the generations to come this burnt offering is to be made regularly at the entrance to the tent of meeting, before the Lord. There I will meet you and speak to you; there also I will meet with the Israelites, and the place will be consecrated by my glory.
- So I will consecrate the tent of meeting and the altar and will consecrate Aaron and his sons to serve me as priests. Then I will dwell among the Israelites and be their God. They will know that I am the Lord their God, who brought them out of Egypt so that I might dwell among them. I am the Lord their God.

The Altar Of Incense
Exodus 30:1 – 30:10

Hippies from the 1970's made burning incense popular. It was used to cover up certain smells that could otherwise get them arrested. But, long before this, people would burn incense for ceremonial purposes. They wanted to create an aroma that would please God.

In these verses, God instructed Moses on how to do it properly:

- Make an altar of acacia wood for burning incense.
- It is to be square, a cubit long and a cubit wide, and two cubits high - its horns of one piece with it. (A cubit was roughly 18 inches.)
- Overlay the top and all the sides and the horns with pure gold, and make a gold molding around it.
- Make two gold rings for the altar below the molding—two on each of the opposite sides—to hold the poles used to carry it.
- Make the poles of acacia wood and overlay them with gold.
- Put the altar in front of the curtain that shields the ark of the covenant law—before the atonement cover that is

over the tablets of the covenant law—where I will meet with you.

- Aaron must burn fragrant incense on the altar every morning when he tends the lamps.
- He must burn incense again when he lights the lamps at twilight so incense will burn regularly before the Lord for the generations to come.
- Do not offer on this altar any other incense or any burnt offering or grain offering, and do not pour a drink offering on it.
- Once a year Aaron shall make atonement on its horns. This annual atonement must be made with the blood of the atoning sin offering for the generations to come. It is most holy to the Lord.

Atonement Money
Exodus 30:11 – 30:16

It takes money to have church services and do ministry. It's just basic economics. The cost of electricity, supplies, and whatever is needed to do God's work is inevitable. Somebody has to pay for it. Many times it's the one heading up the ministry. Unfortunately, some people don't like giving money to things like that – even if they are attending or receiving a benefit from it.

God told Moses to tell the Israelites to pay and called it Atonement Money (a ransom for their life that was spared from Egypt). This money would be used for their service at the tent of meeting. Here's what God told him:

- When you take a census of the Israelites to count them, each one must pay the Lord a ransom for his life at the time he is counted. Then no plague will come on them when you number them.

- Each one who crosses over to those already counted is to give a half shekel, according to the sanctuary shekel, which weighs twenty gerahs. This half shekel is an offering to the Lord. (Money Fact: A gerah is an ancient Hebrew unit of weight and currency which was equivalent to 1/20th of a shekel. God tells Moses, the payment for life ransom during the census taking is 1/2 a shekel (which weighs ten gerahs). This would make a whole shekel equal to 20 gerahs. A half shekel back in the day was silver and weighed about 8 grams. In today's market, this would be worth about 5 dollars. However, back in those days, it was roughly the same as a few days of labor pay.)
- All who cross over, those twenty years old or more, are to give an offering to the Lord.
- The rich are not to give more than a half shekel and the poor are not to give less when you make the offering to the Lord to atone for your lives.
- Receive the atonement money from the Israelites and use it for the service of the tent of meeting. It will be a memorial for the Israelites before the Lord, making atonement for your lives.

Basin For Washing
Exodus 30:17 – 30:21

The priests had to have clean feet and hands before they entered the tent of meeting. They did this by washing with water from a basin at the entrance door. Failure to do so would end in death. God was serious about priests having dirty feet and hands. This is what He instructed Moses to do:

- Make a bronze basin, with its bronze stand, for washing. Place it between the tent of meeting and the altar, and put water in it.
- Aaron and his sons are to wash their hands and feet with water from it.
- Whenever they enter the tent of meeting, they shall wash with water so that they will not die. Also, when they approach the altar to minister by presenting a food offering to the Lord, they shall wash their hands and feet so that they will not die. This is to be a lasting ordinance for Aaron and his descendants for the generations to come.

Anointing Oil
Exodus 30:22 – 30:33

Anointing oil was like a sacred perfume that was used to make things in the tent of meeting holy. It was used to consecrate the priests as well. No one else could use it. I'm sure it smelled good and was probably inviting for someone to wear - maybe a few squirts on their neck or under their arms – to impress their friends. But, God told Moses that only the priests could use it. Anyone else would have to be cut off from their people.

These were the ingredients created by God for the priestly anointing oil and His instructions to Moses on how to use it:

- Take the following fine spices: 500 shekels (12.57 lbs) of liquid myrrh, half as much (that is, 250 shekels – 6.28 lbs) of fragrant cinnamon, 250 shekels (6.28 lbs) of fragrant calamus, 500 shekels (12.57 lbs) of cassia—all according to the sanctuary shekel—and a hin (1.5 gallons) of olive oil. (A shekel was also a unit of weight. 1 shekel was equal to .02513 lbs. 1 hin was equal to 1.5 gallons.)
- Make these into a sacred anointing oil, a fragrant blend, the work of a perfumer. It will be the sacred anointing oil.
- Then use it to anoint the tent of meeting, the ark of the covenant law, the table and all its articles, the lampstand

and its accessories, the altar of incense, the altar of burnt offering and all its utensils, and the basin with its stand. You shall consecrate them so they will be most holy, and whatever touches them will be holy.

- Anoint Aaron and his sons and consecrate them so they may serve me as priests.
- Say to the Israelites, 'This is to be my sacred anointing oil for the generations to come.
- Do not pour it on anyone else's body and do not make any other oil using the same formula. It is sacred, and you are to consider it sacred. Generic band versions were not acceptable.
- Whoever makes perfume like it and puts it on anyone other than a priest must be cut off from their people.

Incense
Exodus 30:34 – 30:38

Incense? God must have liked incense. He wanted Moses to make some and place it in front of the ark of the covenant law in the tent of meeting.

Here's how God instructed Moses to make incense:

- Take fragrant spices—gum resin, onycha and galbanum—and pure frankincense, all in equal amounts, and make a fragrant blend of incense, the work of a perfumer. It is to be salted and pure and sacred.
- Grind some of it to powder and place it in front of the ark of the covenant law in the tent of meeting, where I will meet with you. It shall be most holy to you.

Bezalel And Oholiab

Exodus 31:1 – 31:12

At this point, Moses is probably stressing out. I bet his head was about to explode. God had instructed him to do so much. He had him building stuff, sewing things, turning precious metals and gems into works of art and making perfume. I would almost guarantee you that Moses had never done this kind of stuff before in his life. God knew that. That's why He sent him some help.

Ladies and gentlemen... I introduce to you... Bezalel and Oholiab. Yeah, I know. Their names sound funny.

These would be the main helpers that Moses would need to get all of this stuff produced. God says it right here:

See, I have chosen Bezalel son of Uri, the son of Hur, of the tribe of Judah, and I have filled him with the Spirit of God, with wisdom, with understanding, with knowledge and with all kinds of skills - to make artistic designs for work in gold, silver and bronze, to cut and set stones, to work in wood, and to engage in all kinds of crafts. Moreover, I have appointed Oholiab son of Ahisamak, of the tribe of Dan, to help him. Also I have given ability to all the skilled workers to make the tent of meeting, the ark of the covenant law with the atonement cover on it, and all the other furnishings of the tent - the table and its articles, the pure gold lampstand and all its accessories, the altar of incense, the altar of burnt offering and all its utensils, the basin with its stand - and also the woven garments, both the sacred garments for Aaron the priest and the garments for his sons when they serve as priests, and the anointing oil and fragrant incense for the Holy Place. They are to make them just as I commanded you.

This just goes to show us that God will equip us with everything – including the people - we need to do a service for Him. We shouldn't worry.

The Sabbath
Exodus 31:12 – 31:18

In our world today, Sabbath is reverenced on Saturday. For some, it is on Sunday. We treat it as a day to go to church and do 'Jesus stuff'.

In Moses' day, the Sabbath was a serious day. God considered it holy. The people would work six days a week and rest on this Sabbath day – which meant 'not working and keeping it holy'. According to what I've read, Sabbath began at sundown on Friday and ended at sundown on Saturday. People that chose to work anyway on Sabbath would be separated from their people and put to death. Taking a 'day off' was a command by God Himself.

Imagine what would happen if we observed Sabbath in today's world like they did in the Old Testament days.

Worker: Hey, Boss! I'm leaving early today. It's Friday and it's almost Sabbath.

Boss: Hmm. You've been leaving early every Friday at this time. Maybe it's time to review your salary. It seems to me that you're not giving the company a full week of your time.

Worker: But,...

Boss: Maybe you can make up this time by working on Saturdays instead.

Worker: Mmm... sorry. That's Sabbath, too.

Boss: Oh, really?

It would definitely take some getting used to.

After God finished speaking to Moses on Mount Sinai, He gave him the two tablets of the covenant law. These tablets were made of stone and inscribed by the finger of God.

The Golden Calf

Exodus 32:1 – 33:6

Moses was on Mt Sinai for a long time speaking with God. The Israelites had thought he had vanished. I'm sure they were worried because Moses was their leader and had a one-on-one relationship with God. In their minds, no Moses equals no God. They were doomed.

They decided to go and talk with Aaron, Moses' brother. Since Moses was missing and he probably took God with him, maybe it was time to build a god for them to worship. They convinced Aaron to join them in their plan, so he decided to make them a god from their golden earrings. It was a golden calf – made from handcrafted gold. The people loved it. They went all out and built an altar to it, made offerings and even had a dinner celebration to celebrate their new god.

God was well aware of what was going on and told Moses about it. It was time for Moses to climb down the mountain and straighten out his people. God was angry with them and was about to destroy them, but Moses convinced Him to calm down. He let the Israelites live.

I guess the full extent of what the Israelites had done with the golden calf didn't truly register in Moses' head. He may have climbed down the mountain to see what was happening. And then, when he saw what they had done, he got extremely mad. He took those two stone tablets, that were hot off the Holy Press, and smashed them on the ground. He was furious.

He grabbed that golden calf and burned it in a fire. After that, he grounded it up into a powder and sprinkled it in the water. Then, if that wasn't enough, he made the people drink it. Yeah, I would say he was serious about idol worship... or maybe a little psycho.

Because of their sin, about three thousand people died that day. God also struck the people with a plague. God was mad with them. He told Moses to to tell his people to leave the place they were at and head towards the place He had promised Abraham. God sent angels ahead of them to clear out the people that currently lived there. The only problem with this journey is that God said He would not be with them. He needed time to think. He wanted to decide on how to handle stubborn people such as the Israelites.

The Tent Of Meeting
Exodus 33:7 – 33:11

These verses simply explain the tent of meeting and how people worshiped and how Moses would communicate with God. God would appear as a pillar of cloud. Here's how it all went down (according to the verses):

- And Moses took the tabernacle, and pitched it without the camp, afar off from the camp, and called it the Tabernacle of the congregation. And it came to pass, that every one which sought the Lord went out unto the tabernacle of the congregation, which was without the camp.
- And it came to pass, when Moses went out unto the tabernacle, that all the people rose up, and stood every man at his tent door, and looked after Moses, until he was gone into the tabernacle.
- And it came to pass, as Moses entered into the tabernacle, the cloudy pillar descended, and stood at the door of the tabernacle, and the Lord talked with Moses.
- And all the people saw the cloudy pillar stand at the tabernacle door: and all the people rose up and worshipped, every man in his tent door.
- And the Lord spake unto Moses face to face, as a man speaketh unto his friend. And he turned again into the camp: but his servant Joshua, the son of Nun, a young man, departed not out of the tabernacle.

This wasn't the tabernacle that Chapter 35 talks about. This was a tent that was for the sole purpose of Moses. This was where he talked with God. From what these verses say, the people watched Moses as he talked with God. God was with him and spoke to him as a friend. I thought that was cool.

Moses And The Glory Of The Lord
Exodus 33:12 – 33:23

God wasn't happy with the Israelites. The moment they felt that their leader, Moses, had gone missing, they turned their backs on God and started worshiping idols. They had forgotten all that God had done for them, the miracles they had seen Him do and they had experienced. God wasn't happy at all. He wanted them to continue their journey without Him. Moses knew this wasn't a good idea and, in these verses, he pleaded with God. He knew their need for Him in their life's journey.

These verses are a conversation between God and Moses:

Moses: *See, thou sayest unto me, Bring up this people: and thou hast not let me know whom thou wilt send with me. Yet thou hast said, I know thee by name, and thou hast also found grace in my sight. Now therefore, I pray thee, if I have found grace in thy sight, shew me now thy way, that I may know thee, that I may find grace in thy sight: and consider that this nation is thy people.*

God: *My presence shall go with thee, and I will give thee rest.*

Moses: *If thy presence go not with me, carry us not up hence. For wherein shall it be known here that I and thy people have found* grace in thy sight? is it not in that thou goest with us? so shall we be separated, I and thy people, from all the people that are upon the face of the earth.

God: *I will do this thing also that thou hast spoken: for thou hast found grace in my sight, and I know thee by name.*

Moses: *I beseech thee, shew me thy glory.*

God: *I will make all my goodness pass before thee, and I will proclaim the name of the LORD before thee; and will be gracious to whom I will be gracious, and will shew mercy on whom I will shew mercy. And he said, Thou canst not see my face: for there shall no man see me, and live.*

<Moses may have been in shock>

God: *Behold, there is a place by me, and thou shalt stand upon a rock: And it shall come to pass, while my glory passeth by, that I will put thee in a clift of the rock, and will cover thee with my hand while I pass by: And I will take away mine hand, and thou shalt see my back parts: but my face shall not be seen.*

God agrees to be with them on their journey because of Moses' plea. However, they would not be able to see His face. Undoubtedly, by doing so, it would cause them to die. It could have been a shocking experience to see the face of our Creator. Their hearts may have stopped beating out of fear or because of the extreme awesomeness. Who knows?

The New Stone Tablets
Exodus 34:1 – 34:28

As we already know, Moses broke the first set of stone tablets that God had written on. Out of anger at the Israelites, Moses threw them and smashed them into little pieces. Luckily, no one was hurt. In these verses, God is going to allow Moses to create some new ones. In addition, God makes a covenant with the people and adds a few commands for them to follow. Here's how it went down:

And the Lord said unto Moses,
Hew thee two tables of stone
like unto the first: and I will write upon these tables the words that were in the first tables, which thou brakest. And be ready in the morning, and come up in the morning unto mount Sinai, and present thyself there to me in the top of the mount. And no man shall come up with thee, neither let any man be seen throughout all the mount; neither let the flocks nor herds feed before that mount.

And he hewed two tables of stone like unto the first; and Moses rose up early in the morning, and went up unto mount Sinai, as the Lord had commanded him, and took in his hand the two tables of stone. And the Lord descended in the cloud, and stood with him there, and proclaimed the name of the Lord. And the Lord passed by before him, and proclaimed, The Lord, The Lord

God, merciful and gracious, longsuffering, and abundant in goodness and truth, Keeping mercy for thousands, forgiving iniquity and transgression and sin, and that will by no means clear the guilty; visiting the iniquity of the fathers upon the children, and upon the children's children, unto the third and to the fourth generation.

And Moses made haste, and bowed his head toward the earth, and worshipped. And he said, If now I have found grace in thy sight, O Lord, let my Lord, I pray thee, go among us; for it is a stiffnecked people; and pardon our iniquity and our sin, and take us for thine inheritance.

And he said, Behold, I make a covenant: before all thy people I will do marvels, such as have not been done in all the earth, nor in any nation: and all the people among which thou art shall see the work of the Lord: for it is a terrible thing that I will do with thee.

Observe thou that which I command thee this day: behold, I drive out before thee the Amorite, and the Canaanite, and the Hittite, and the Perizzite, and the Hivite, and the Jebusite. Take heed to thyself, lest thou make a covenant with the inhabitants of the land whither thou goest, lest it be for a snare in the midst of thee: But ye shall destroy their altars, break their images, and cut down their groves: For thou shalt worship no other god: for the Lord, whose name is Jealous, is a jealous God: Lest thou make a covenant with the inhabitants of the land, and they go a whoring after their gods, and do sacrifice unto their gods, and one call thee, and thou eat of his sacrifice; And thou take of their daughters unto thy sons, and their daughters go a whoring after their gods, and make thy sons go a whoring after their gods. Thou shalt make thee no molten gods.

The feast of unleavened bread shalt thou keep. Seven days thou shalt eat unleavened bread, as I commanded thee, in the time of the month Abib: for in the month Abib thou camest out from Egypt. All that openeth the matrix is mine; and every firstling among thy cattle, whether ox or sheep, that is male. But the firstling of an ass thou shalt redeem with a lamb: and if thou redeem him not, then shalt thou break his neck. All the firstborn of thy sons thou shalt redeem. And none shall appear before me empty. Six days thou shalt work, but on the seventh day thou shalt rest: in earing time and in harvest thou shalt rest. And thou shalt observe the feast of weeks, of the firstfruits of wheat harvest, and the feast of ingathering at the year's end. Thrice in the year shall all your men children appear before the Lord God, the God of Israel. For I will cast out the nations before thee, and enlarge thy borders: neither shall any man desire thy land, when thou shalt go up to appear before the Lord thy God thrice in the year. Thou shalt not offer the blood of my sacrifice with leaven; neither shall the sacrifice of the feast of the passover be left unto the morning. The first of the firstfruits of thy land thou shalt bring unto the house of the Lord thy God. Thou shalt not seethe a kid in his mother's milk. And the Lord said unto Moses, Write thou these words: for after the tenor of these words I have made a covenant with thee and with Israel.

And he was there with the Lord forty days and forty nights; he did neither eat bread, nor drink water. And he wrote upon the tables the words of the covenant, the ten commandments.

Basically, to sum up all of these verses, Moses meets up with God on Mount Sinai with another set of stone tablets. Remember, Moses broke the first ones. God writes the Ten Commandments on them... again. After that, it seems that God makes a covenant with the Israelites and delivers some ceremonial expectations that the Israelites should follow. This all happened in the forty days that Moses spent up there on that mountain.

An interesting thing that caught my attention from these verses is the word 'matrix'. These verse says 'openeth the matrix'. Matrix is a word you hear in the movies – usually science fiction – or from one of them brainy nerd people at Comic Conventions. But, today we hear it here... in the Bible. What's that all about?

The phrase 'openeth the matrix' is mentioned five times in the King James version of the Bible. For reference, here they are:

Exodus 13:12
Exodus 13:15
Exodus 34:19
Numbers 3:12
Numbers 18:15

Before we get all weird and scientific, the word 'matrix' basically means 'womb' – the place where babies are born. That's it - nothing more.

The Radiant Face Of Moses

Exodus 34:29 – 34:35

Moses had a glow on his face
after talking with God. It was
noticeable by the people, but
not by Moses. He was
unaware. All he knew was that
people were afraid to be near
him. Here's what the verses
have to say:

*And it came to pass, when
Moses came down from mount
Sinai with the two tables of
testimony in Moses' hand,
when he came down from the
mount, that Moses wist not
that the skin of his face shone
while he talked with him. And
when Aaron and all the children of Israel saw Moses, behold, the
skin of his face shone; and they were afraid to come nigh him.
And Moses called unto them; and Aaron and all the rulers of the
congregation returned unto him: and Moses talked with them.*

*And afterward all the children of Israel came nigh: and he gave
them in commandment all that the Lord had spoken with him in
mount Sinai. And till Moses had done speaking with them, he put
a vail on his face. But when Moses went in before the Lord to
speak with him, he took the vail off, until he came out. And he
came out, and spake unto the children of Israel that which he
was commanded. And the children of Israel saw the face of
Moses, that the skin of Moses' face shone: and Moses put the
vail upon his face again, until he went in to speak with him.*

Moses had a noticeable glow to his face. Actually, it was quite scary. People didn't want to be around him. I guess he became a little self-conscious about it, so he put a veil over his face when he told them of all that God said to him on the mountain. The Bible doesn't say how long this facial glow lasted, but I imagine it was kinda weird to look at.

Sabbath Regulations
Exodus 35:1 – 35:3

God was serious about the Sabbath Day. Moses tells the people what God told him:

And Moses gathered all the congregation of the children of Israel together, and said unto them, These are the words which the Lord hath commanded, that ye should do them. Six days shall work be done, but on the seventh day there shall be to you an

holy day, a sabbath of rest to the Lord: whosoever doeth work therein shall be put to death. Ye shall kindle no fire throughout your habitations upon the sabbath day.

The Sabbath Day regulations had already been mentioned in previous verses, but this one had an extra line item. They couldn't 'kindle a fire in their homes' on the Sabbath. I'm sure fire was important back then because I don't think electricity was invented yet. Fire was probably used for lighting, heating and cooking. Were they not allowed to do any of this? All it says is that they weren't allowed to work. Maybe they had to throw a few extra logs on the fire a few seconds before Sabbath so that it would burn for 24 hours? Who knows?

Material For The Tabernacle
Exodus 35:4 – 35:29

This was the list of materials that would be needed for building the tabernacle. It was quite specific in details. Moses told the crowd what he would need and left it up to them to bring it. He didn't make demands from everybody. He let them decide on whether they wanted to be part of it or not. They had to give from the heart. Here's what the verses say:

And Moses spake unto all the congregation of the children of Israel, saying, This is the thing which the Lord commanded, saying, Take ye from among you an offering unto the Lord: whosoever is of a willing heart, let him bring it, an offering of the Lord; gold, and silver, and brass, And blue, and purple, and scarlet, and fine linen, and goats' hair, And rams' skins dyed red, and badgers' skins, and shittim wood, And oil for the light, and spices for anointing oil, and for the sweet incense, And onyx stones, and stones to be set for the ephod, and for the breastplate. And every wise hearted among you shall come, and make all that the Lord hath commanded; The

tabernacle, his tent, and his covering, his taches, and his boards, his bars, his pillars, and his sockets, The ark, and the staves thereof, with the mercy seat, and the vail of the covering, The table, and his staves, and all his vessels, and the shewbread, The candlestick also for the light, and his furniture, and his lamps, with the oil for the light, And the incense altar, and his staves, and the anointing oil, and the sweet incense, and the hanging for the door at the entering in of the tabernacle, The altar of burnt offering, with his brasen grate, his staves, and all his vessels, the laver and his foot, The hangings of the court, his pillars, and their sockets, and the hanging for the door of the court, The pins of the tabernacle, and the pins of the court, and their cords, The cloths of service, to do service in the holy place, the holy garments for Aaron the priest, and the garments of his sons, to minister in the priest's office. And all the congregation of the children of Israel departed from the presence of Moses.

And they came, every one whose heart stirred him up, and every one whom his spirit made willing, and they brought the Lord's offering to the work of the tabernacle of the congregation, and for all his service, and for the holy garments. And they came, both men and women, as many as were willing hearted, and brought bracelets, and earrings, and rings, and tablets, all jewels of gold: and every man that offered offered an offering of gold unto the Lord. And every man, with whom was found blue, and purple, and scarlet, and fine linen, and goats' hair, and red skins of rams, and badgers' skins, brought them. Every one that did offer an offering of silver and brass brought the Lord's offering: and every man, with whom was found shittim wood for any work of the service, brought it. And all the women that were wise hearted did spin with their hands, and brought that which they had spun, both of blue, and of purple, and of scarlet, and of fine linen. And all the women whose heart stirred them up in wisdom spun goats' hair. And the rulers brought onyx stones, and stones to be set, for the ephod, and for the breastplate; And spice, and oil for the light, and for the anointing oil, and for the sweet incense. The children of Israel brought a willing offering unto the Lord, every man and woman, whose heart made them willing to bring for all manner of work, which the Lord had commanded to be made by the hand of Moses.

Bezalel And Oholiab
Exodus 35:30 – 36:7

Moses had a big job to do and probably wondered how he would get it all done. He was just one person with only so much daylight and skills to make it happen. I'm sure the people wondered how all of these detailed projects God had placed on them could possibly become reality. But, God had supplied – as He always does – them with two skilled people to coordinate the whole project. Their name was Bezalel and Oholiab.

According to the scriptures:

And Moses said unto the children of Israel, See, the Lord hath called by name Bezaleel the son of Uri, the son of Hur, of the tribe of Judah; And he hath filled him with the spirit of God, in wisdom, in understanding, and in knowledge, and in all manner of workmanship; And to devise curious works, to work in gold, and in silver, and in brass, And in the cutting of stones, to set them, and in carving of wood, to make any manner of cunning work. And he hath put in his heart that he may teach, both he, and Aholiab, the son of Ahisamach, of the tribe of Dan. Them hath he filled with wisdom of heart, to work all manner of work, of the engraver, and of the cunning workman, and of the embroiderer, in blue, and in purple, in scarlet, and in fine linen, and of the weaver, even of them that do any work, and of those that devise cunning work.

Then wrought Bezaleel and Aholiab, and every wise hearted man, in whom the Lord put wisdom and understanding to know how to work all manner of work for the service of the sanctuary, according to all that the Lord had commanded. And Moses called Bezaleel and Aholiab, and every wise hearted man, in whose heart the Lord had put wisdom, even every one whose heart stirred him up to come unto the work to do it: And they received of Moses all the offering, which the children of Israel had brought for the work of the service of the sanctuary, to make it withal. And they brought yet unto him free offerings every morning. And all the wise men, that wrought all the work of the sanctuary, came every man from his work which they made;

And they spake unto Moses, saying, The people bring much more than enough for the service of the work, which the Lord commanded to make. And Moses gave commandment, and they caused it to be proclaimed throughout the camp, saying, Let neither man nor woman make any more work for the offering of the sanctuary. So the people were restrained from bringing. For the stuff they had was sufficient for all the work to make it, and too much.

It sounds like Moses received enough materials from the people to get the job done. Actually, he had more than enough and had to stop them from bringing any more.

The Tabernacle
Exodus 36:8 – 36:38

Making cloth back in those days was a tedious job. No, you couldn't go to your local fabric shop chain and buy it. I get the feeling this was all done by hand by highly skilled professionals. Actually the entire job was done by people highly skilled in their trade. Here's what the scriptures had to say:

And every wise hearted man among them that wrought the work of the tabernacle made ten curtains of fine twined linen, and blue, and purple, and scarlet: with cherubims of cunning work made he them. The length of one curtain was twenty and eight cubits, and the breadth of one curtain four cubits: the curtains were all of one size. And he coupled the five curtains one unto another: and the other five curtains he coupled one unto another. And he made loops of blue on the edge of one curtain from the selvedge in the coupling: likewise he made in the uttermost side of another curtain, in the coupling of the second. Fifty loops made he in one curtain, and fifty loops made he in the edge of the curtain which was in the coupling of the second: the loops held one curtain to another.

And he made fifty taches of gold, and coupled the curtains one unto another with the taches: so it became one tabernacle. And he made curtains of goats' hair for the tent over the tabernacle: eleven curtains he made them. The length of one curtain was thirty cubits, and four cubits was the breadth of one curtain: the eleven curtains were of one size. And he coupled five curtains by themselves, and six curtains by themselves. And he made fifty loops upon the uttermost edge of the curtain in the coupling, and fifty loops made he upon the edge of the curtain which coupleth the second. And he made fifty taches of brass to couple the tent together, that it might be one. And he made a covering for the tent of rams' skins dyed red, and a covering of badgers' skins above that. And he made boards for the tabernacle of shittim wood, standing up. The length of a board was ten cubits, and the breadth of a board one cubit and a half. One board had two tenons, equally distant one from another: thus did he make for all the boards of the tabernacle. And he made boards for the tabernacle; twenty boards for the south side southward: And forty sockets of silver he made under the twenty boards; two sockets under one board for his two tenons, and two sockets under another board for his two tenons. And for the other side of the tabernacle, which is toward the north corner, he made twenty boards, And their forty sockets of silver; two sockets under one board, and two sockets under another board. And for the sides of the tabernacle westward he made six boards. And two boards made he for the corners of the tabernacle in the two sides. And they were coupled beneath, and coupled together at the head thereof, to one ring: thus he did to both of them in both the corners. And there were eight boards; and their sockets were sixteen sockets of silver, under every board two sockets.

And he made bars of shittim wood; five for the boards of the one side of the tabernacle, And five bars for the boards of the other side of the tabernacle, and five bars for the boards of the *tabernacle for the sides westward. And he made the middle bar to shoot through the boards from the one end to the other. And he overlaid the boards with gold, and made their rings of gold to be places for the bars, and overlaid the bars with gold. And he made a vail of blue, and purple, and scarlet, and fine twined linen: with cherubims made he it of cunning work. And he made thereunto four pillars of shittim wood, and overlaid them with gold: their hooks were of gold; and he cast for them four sockets of silver. And he made an hanging for the tabernacle door of blue, and purple, and scarlet, and fine twined linen, of needlework; And the five pillars of it with their hooks: and he overlaid their chapiters and their fillets with gold: but their five sockets were of brass.*

For the record, cherubim are mighty angels. I just thought I would put that out there.

The Ark
Exodus 37:1 – 37:9

The ark was built to hold the Ten Commandments. It symbolized God's covenant with His people. The ark was Israel's most sacred object and was kept in the Most Holy Place in the tabernacle. Here's how the scriptures say it was built:

And Bezaleel made the ark of shittim wood: two cubits and a half was the length of it, and a cubit and a half the breadth of it, and a cubit and a half the height of it: And he overlaid it with pure gold within and without, and made a crown of gold to it round about. And he cast for it four rings of gold, to be set by the four corners of it; even two rings upon the one side of it, and two rings upon the other side of it. And he made staves of shittim wood, and overlaid them with gold. And he put the staves into the rings by the sides of the ark, to bear the ark.

134

And he made the mercy seat of pure gold: two cubits and a half was the length thereof, and one cubit and a half the breadth thereof. And he made two cherubims of gold, beaten out of one piece made he them, on the two ends of the mercy seat; One cherub on the end on this side, and another cherub on the other end on that side: out of the mercy seat made he the cherubims on the two ends thereof. And the cherubims spread out their wings on high, and covered with their wings over the mercy seat, with their faces one to another; even to the mercy seatward were the faces of the cherubims.

The Table
Exodus 37:10 – 37:16

The scriptures are self-explanatory:

And he made the table of shittim wood: two cubits was the length thereof, and a cubit the breadth thereof, and a cubit and a half the height thereof: And he overlaid it with pure gold, and made thereunto a crown of gold round about. Also he made thereunto a border of an handbreadth round about; and made a crown of gold for the border thereof round about. And he cast for it four rings of gold, and put the rings upon the four corners that were in the four feet thereof. Over against the border were the rings, the places for the staves to bear the table. And he made the staves of shittim wood, and overlaid them with gold, to bear the table. And he made the vessels which were upon the table, his dishes, and his spoons, and his bowls, and his covers to cover withal, of pure gold.

I have never heard of shittim wood, but from what I've read, it's basically the same as acacia wood. It's a hard durable wood that lasts a long time. Plus, it was accented with gold and even the accessories were made from gold, too. This table was built to last.

The Lampstand
Exodus 37:17 – 37:24

The lampstand was very detailed and probably expensive to make. Here's what the scriptures say:

And he made the candlestick of pure gold: of beaten work made he the candlestick; his shaft, and his branch, his bowls, his knops, and his flowers, were of the same: And six branches going out of the sides thereof; three branches of the candlestick out of the one side thereof, and three branches of the candlestick out of the other side thereof: Three bowls made after the fashion of almonds in one branch, a knop and a flower; and three bowls made like almonds in another branch, a knop and a flower: so throughout the six branches going out of the candlestick. And in the candlestick were four bowls made like almonds, his knops, and his flowers: And a knop under two branches of the same, and a knop under two branches of the same, and a knop under two branches of the same, according to the six branches going out of it. Their knops and their branches were of the same: all of it was one beaten work of pure gold. And he made his seven lamps, and his snuffers, and his snuffdishes, of pure gold. Of a talent of pure gold made he it, and all the vessels thereof.

The Altar Of Incense
Exodus 37:25 – 37:29

The scriptures sum it all up:

And he made the incense altar of shittim wood: the length of it was a cubit, and the breadth of it a cubit; it was foursquare; and two cubits was the height of it; the horns thereof were of the same. And he overlaid it with pure gold, both the top of it, and the sides thereof round about, and the horns of it: also he made unto it a crown of gold round about. And he made two rings of gold for it under the crown thereof, by the two corners of it, upon the two sides thereof, to be places for the staves to bear it withal. And he made the staves of shittim wood, and overlaid them with gold. And he made the holy anointing oil, and the pure incense of sweet spices, according to the work of the apothecary.

It appears that this altar was roughly 1.5 feet x 1.5 feet and 3 feet tall. That doesn't sound like a big altar, but it was for burning incense, so I don't think you would need too much space. It was decked out in gold and probably looked fancy. It was definitely an eye-catcher.

The Altar Of Burnt Offering
Exodus 38:1 – 38:7

Altar building according to the scriptures:

And he made the altar of burnt offering of shittim wood: five cubits was the length thereof, and five cubits the breadth thereof; it was foursquare; and three cubits the height thereof.

And he made the horns thereof on the four corners of it; the horns thereof were of the same: and he overlaid it with brass. And he made all the vessels of the altar, the pots, and the shovels, and the basons, and the fleshhooks, and the firepans: all the vessels thereof made he of brass. And he made for the altar a brasen grate of network under the compass thereof beneath unto the midst of it. And he cast four rings for the four ends of the grate of brass, to be places for the staves. And he made the staves of shittim wood, and overlaid them with brass. And he put the staves into the rings on the sides of the altar, to bear it withal; he made the altar hollow with boards.

This altar was big in size. It was roughly 7.5 feet x 7.5 feet and 4.5 feet tall. This was bigger than your normal dining room table. It was even covered in brass. That would make it a very nice furniture piece for putting burned dead animals on.

Basin For Washing
Exodus 38:8

Even the sink had to be special-made.

And he made the laver of brass, and the foot of it of brass, of the lookingglasses of the women assembling, which assembled at the door of the tabernacle of the congregation.

This sink was made from shiny polished brass. I bet it was beautiful. The purpose was for simply washing feet and hands. I imagine someone had the hard task of keeping this thing cleaned. Can you imagine how hard that would have been?

The Courtyard
Exodus 38:9 – 38:20

And he made the court: on the south side southward the hangings of the court were of fine twined linen, an hundred cubits: Their pillars were twenty, and their brasen sockets twenty; the hooks of the pillars and their fillets were of silver.

And for the north side the hangings were an hundred cubits, their pillars were twenty, and their sockets of brass twenty; the hooks of the pillars and their fillets of silver.

And for the west side were hangings of fifty cubits, their pillars ten, and their sockets ten; the hooks of the pillars and their fillets of silver.

And for the east side eastward fifty cubits. The hangings of the one side of the gate were fifteen cubits; their pillars three, and their sockets three.

And for the other side of the court gate, on this hand and that hand, were hangings of fifteen cubits; their pillars three, and their sockets three. All the hangings of the court round about were of fine twined linen. And the sockets for the pillars were of brass; the hooks of the pillars and their fillets of silver; and the overlaying of their chapiters of silver; and all the pillars of the court were filleted with silver. And the hanging for the gate of the court was needlework, of blue, and purple, and scarlet, and fine twined linen: and twenty cubits was the length, and the height in the breadth was five cubits, answerable to the hangings of the court. And their pillars were four, and their sockets of brass four; their hooks of silver, and the overlaying of their chapiters and their fillets of silver. And all the pins of the tabernacle, and of the court round about, were of brass.

The courtyard had a lot of pillars and hanging curtains. It was huge. The hangings on the north and south side were roughly 150 feet each. The east and west side had hangings that were 50 feet each. The average sized home in the U.S. is roughly 25 feet wide by 50 feet long. If my math is correct, you could easily fit 6 homes inside this courtyard. That's massive.

The Materials Used
Exodus 38:21 – 38:31

Moses was the boss, but Ithamar and Bezaleel directed the whole project. And it seems that someone was keeping records of the material used. It looks like everything was recorded. Here's what the scriptures say:

This is the sum of the tabernacle, even of the tabernacle of testimony, as it was counted, according to the commandment of Moses, for the service of the Levites, by the hand of Ithamar, son to Aaron the priest. And Bezaleel the son of Uri, the son of Hur, of the tribe of Judah, made all that the LORD commanded Moses. And with him was Aholiab, son of Ahisamach, of the tribe of Dan, an engraver, and a cunning workman, and an embroiderer in blue, and in purple, and in scarlet, and fine linen.

All the gold that was occupied for the work in all the work of the holy place, even the gold of the offering, was twenty and nine talents, and seven hundred and thirty shekels, after the shekel of the sanctuary. And the silver of them that were numbered of the congregation was an hundred talents, and a thousand seven hundred and threescore and fifteen shekels, after the shekel of the sanctuary: A bekah for every man, that is, half a shekel, after the shekel of the sanctuary, for every one that went to be numbered, from twenty years old and upward, for six hundred thousand and three thousand and five hundred and fifty men. And of the hundred talents of silver were cast the sockets of the sanctuary, and the sockets of the vail; an hundred sockets of the hundred talents, a talent for a socket. And of the thousand seven hundred seventy and five shekels he made hooks for the pillars, and overlaid their chapiters, and filleted them. And the brass of the offering was seventy talents, and two thousand and four hundred shekels. And therewith he made the sockets to the door of the tabernacle of the congregation, and the brasen altar, and the brasen grate for it, and all the vessels of the altar, And the sockets of the court round about, and the sockets of the court gate, and all the pins of the tabernacle, and all the pins of the court round about.

All of the materials were donated by people that just wanted to share what they owned with Moses and his God-given project. Everything was freely given. Actually, there was so much stuff given that Moses had to tell them that they were no longer accepting donations. They had an over-abundance. The cool thing from reading these verses is that someone kept a list of what actually got used. Someone kept count.

Maybe this person was an accountant and was keeping records for tax purposes, but I seriously doubt it. Or maybe, since everything was given, they kept a record to assure people that their donation wasn't mishandled.

I mean, in today's world, your donation to a ministry isn't guaranteed to be used towards their ministry efforts. Some ministry leaders put it in their own pockets and use it for personal use. It happens.

The Priestly Garments
Exodus 39:1

The priests wore special clothes:

And of the blue, and purple, and scarlet, they made cloths of service, to do service in the holy place, and made the holy garments for Aaron; as the Lord commanded Moses.

You could always tell who the priest was because his clothes would be colored blue, purple and orange-ish red. He may have looked like a player on a college football team. But, hey! At least a priest stood out. He wouldn't look like everyone else.

The Ephod
Exodus 39:2 – 39:7

An ephod was a sleeveless garment worn by the Jewish priests:

And he made the ephod of gold, blue, and purple, and scarlet, and fine twined linen. And they did beat the gold into thin plates, and cut it into wires, to work it in the blue, and in the purple, and in the scarlet, and in the fine linen, with cunning work. They made shoulderpieces for it, to couple it together: by the two edges was it coupled together. And the curious girdle of his ephod, that was upon it, was of the same, according to the work thereof; of gold, blue, and purple, and scarlet, and fine twined linen; as the Lord commanded Moses. And they wrought onyx stones inclosed in ouches of gold, graven, as signets are graven, with the names of the children of Israel. And he put them on the shoulders of the ephod, that they should be stones for a memorial to the children of Israel; as the Lord commanded Moses.

This ephod was blue, purple and orange-ish red with gold. It had shoulder pads and a girdle. It also had onyx stones on it that contained the names of the children of Israel. I bet this thing was uncomfortable and heavy to wear. But, I bet it looked good.

The Breastpiece
Exodus 39:8 – 39:21

If wearing the ephod wasn't enough, the priest also wore a breastpiece:

And he made the breastplate of cunning work, like the work of the ephod; of gold, blue, and purple, and scarlet, and fine twined linen. It was foursquare; they made the breastplate double: a span was the length thereof, and a span the breadth thereof, being doubled. And they set in it four rows of stones: the first row was a sardius, a topaz, and a carbuncle: this was the first row. And the second row, an emerald, a sapphire, and a diamond. And the third row, a ligure, an agate, and an amethyst. And the fourth row, a beryl, an onyx, and a jasper: they were inclosed in ouches of gold in their inclosings. And the stones were according to the names of the children of Israel, twelve, according to their names, like the engravings of a signet, every one with his name, according to the twelve tribes. And they made upon the breastplate chains at the ends, of wreathen work of pure gold. And they made two ouches of gold, and two gold rings; and put the two rings in the two ends of the breastplate. And they put the two wreathen chains of gold in the two rings on the ends of the breastplate.

And the two ends of the two wreathen chains they fastened in the two ouches, and put them on the shoulderpieces of the ephod, before it. And they made two rings of gold, and put them on the two ends of the breastplate, upon the border of it, which was on the side of the ephod inward. And they made two other golden rings, and put them on the two sides of the ephod underneath, toward the forepart of it, over against the other coupling thereof, above the curious girdle of the ephod. And they did bind the breastplate by his rings unto the rings of the ephod with a lace of blue, that it might be above the curious girdle of the ephod, and that the breastplate might not be loosed from the ephod; as the Lord commanded Moses.

THE LEWIS GUIDE
READERS

It sounds like the breastpiece was made similar to the ephod, but with more stones and more gold. Even though the Bible doesn't say how much all of these priestly clothes weighed, I would have to guess it was pretty heavy. Hopefully, they didn't have to wear it all day.

Other Priestly Garments
Exodus 39:22 – 39:31

By this point, I am feeling sorry for the priests back in the day. They wore fancy clothes that probably weighed enough to cause them back problems. So far, we know the priests wore an ephod and a breastpiece. But according to these verses, they also wore robes and a crown:

And he made the robe of the ephod of woven work, all of blue. And there was an hole in the midst of the robe, as the hole of an habergeon, with a band round about the hole, that it should not rend. And they made upon the hems of the robe pomegranates of blue, and purple, and scarlet, and twined linen. And they made bells of pure gold, and put the bells between the pomegranates upon the hem of the robe, round about between the pomegranates; A bell and a pomegranate, a bell and a pomegranate, round about the hem of the robe to minister in; as the Lord commanded Moses. And they made coats of fine linen of woven work for Aaron, and for his sons, And a mitre of fine linen, and goodly bonnets of fine linen, and linen breeches of fine twined linen, And a girdle of fine twined linen, and blue, and purple, and scarlet, of needlework; as the Lord commanded Moses. And they made the plate of the holy crown of pure gold, and wrote upon it a writing, like to the engravings of a signet, HOLINESS TO THE LORD. And they tied unto it a lace of blue, to fasten it on high upon the mitre; as the Lord commanded Moses.

RING-A-LING -A-LING!

HEAR THAT? THAT WAS A PRIEST... OR MAYBE A COW. NOT SURE.

THE LEWIS GUIDE READERS

The robes were probably beautiful works of art, especially with the golden bells attached to them. That tells me that these robes made sounds every time a priest walked. Not only could you spot a priest in a crowd with their flashy colors, but you could also hear them. I bet that was cool.

And to top it all off, the priests wore crowns of gold. I'm sure priests were considered very special people back in those days.

Moses Inspects The Tabernacle
Exodus 39:32 – 39:43

Moses was a good leader and was able to delegate very well. He had built everything according to the strict details that God had commanded. The people that worked on this project did a great job.

Thus was all the work of the tabernacle of the tent of the congregation finished: and the children of Israel did according to all that the Lord commanded Moses, so did they. And they brought the tabernacle unto Moses, the tent, and all his furniture, his taches, his boards, his bars, and his pillars, and his sockets, And the covering of rams' skins dyed red, and the covering of badgers' skins, and the vail of the covering, The ark of the testimony, and the staves thereof, and the mercy seat, The table, and all the vessels thereof, and the shewbread, The pure candlestick, with the lamps thereof, even with the lamps to be set in order, and all the vessels thereof, and the oil for light, And the golden altar, and the anointing oil, and the sweet incense, and the hanging for the tabernacle door, The brasen altar, and his grate of brass, his staves, and all his vessels, the laver and his foot, The hangings of the court, his pillars, and his sockets, and the hanging for the court gate, his cords, and his pins, and all the vessels of the service of the tabernacle, for the tent of the congregation, The cloths of service to do service in the holy place, and the holy garments for Aaron the priest, and his sons' garments, to minister in the priest's office.

According to all that the Lord commanded Moses, so the children of Israel made all the work. And Moses did look upon all the work, and, behold, they had done it as the Lord had commanded, even so had they done it: and Moses blessed them.

The children of Israel brought all that they had made to show to Moses. Moses was impressed and blessed them. Everything was up to code and made to spec.

Setting Up The Tabernacle
Exodus 40:1 – 40:33

The tabernacle and all of it's accessories were built. Now it was time to put it all to use. God gave Moses instructions on how it should be done:

And the Lord spake unto Moses, saying,

On the first day of the first month shalt thou set up the tabernacle of the tent of the congregation. And thou shalt put therein the ark of the testimony, and cover the ark with the vail. And thou shalt bring in the table, and set in order the things that are to be set in order upon it; and thou shalt bring in the candlestick, and light the lamps thereof. And thou shalt set the altar of gold for the incense before the ark of the testimony, and put the hanging of the door to the tabernacle. And thou shalt set the altar of the burnt offering before the door of the tabernacle of the tent of the congregation. And thou shalt set the laver between the tent of the congregation and the altar, and shalt put water therein. And thou shalt set up the court round about, and hang up the hanging at the court gate. And thou shalt take the anointing oil, and anoint the tabernacle, and all that is therein, and shalt hallow it, and all the vessels thereof: and it shall be holy. And thou shalt anoint the altar of the burnt offering, and all his vessels, and sanctify the altar: and it shall be an altar most holy. And thou shalt anoint the laver and his foot, and sanctify it. And thou shalt bring Aaron and his sons unto the door of the tabernacle of the congregation, and wash them with water. And thou shalt put upon Aaron the holy garments, and anoint him, and sanctify him; that he may minister unto me in the priest's office. And thou shalt bring his sons, and clothe them with coats: And thou shalt anoint them, as thou didst anoint their father, that they may minister unto me in the priest's office: for their anointing shall surely be an everlasting priesthood throughout their generations.

Thus did Moses: according to all that the Lord commanded him, so did he. And it came to pass in the first month in the second year, on the first day of the month, that the tabernacle was reared up. And Moses reared up the tabernacle, and fastened his sockets, and set up the boards thereof, and put in the bars thereof, and reared up his pillars. And he spread abroad the tent over the tabernacle, and put the covering of the tent above upon it; as the Lord commanded Moses. And he took and put the testimony into the ark, and set the staves on the ark, and put the mercy seat above upon the ark: And he brought the ark into the tabernacle, and set up the vail of the covering, and covered the ark of the testimony; as the Lord commanded Moses. And he put the table in the tent of the congregation, upon the side of the tabernacle northward, without the vail. And he set the bread in order upon it before the Lord; as the Lord had commanded Moses. And he put the candlestick in the tent of the congregation, over against the table, on the side of the tabernacle southward. And he lighted the lamps before the Lord; as the Lord commanded Moses. And he put the golden altar in the tent of the congregation before the vail: And he burnt sweet incense thereon; as the Lord commanded Moses. And he set up the hanging at the door of the tabernacle. And he put the altar of burnt offering by the door of the tabernacle of the tent of the *congregation, and offered upon it the burnt offering and the meat offering; as the Lord commanded Moses. And he set the laver between the tent of the congregation and the altar, and put water there, to wash withal. And Moses and Aaron and his sons washed their hands and their feet thereat: When they went into the tent of the congregation, and when they came near unto the altar, they washed; as the Lord commanded Moses. And he reared up the court round about the tabernacle and the altar, and set up the hanging of the court gate. So Moses finished the work.*

HOW ABOUT THAT DRAWING OF THE TABERNACLE?

TABERNACLE

THE LEWIS GUIDE READERS

Even though this tabernacle was huge, it was also portable. According to the verses, the people of Israel would set it up once a year on the first day of the first month. On this day, they would worship and make offerings to God.

There's a life-size replica of the ancient tabernacle currently in Israel that is set up for tourists (Jewish and Christian). It has been made to look like the one that Moses built. After reading Exodus and learning about the tabernacle, it might be cool to visit it and see it in real life.

The Glory Of The Lord
Exodus 40:34 – 40:38

The tabernacle was a huge portable tent that God told Moses to build. He gave him the building instructions, furnished the skilled people to do the work, provided the materials and it all turned out great. Moses liked it and I think God was impressed, too. God dwelled with the Israelites there in that tabernacle.

They would always know that His presence was with them because God made it known through a pillar of cloud and fire. They could see this.

Then a cloud covered the tent of the congregation, and the glory of the Lord filled the tabernacle. And Moses was not able to enter into the tent of the congregation, because the cloud abode thereon, and the glory of the Lord filled the tabernacle. And when the cloud was taken up from over the tabernacle, the children of Israel went onward in all their journeys: But if the cloud were not taken up, then they journeyed not till the day that it was taken up. For the cloud of the Lord was upon the tabernacle by day, and fire was on it by night, in the sight of all the house of Israel, throughout all their journeys.

As the Israelites journeyed to the Promised Land, they would use the pillar of cloud and fire to lead the way. This was God directing them. The same can be applied to us today. Jesus is the light of the world.

Then spake Jesus again unto them, saying, I am the light of the world: he that followeth me shall not walk in darkness, but shall have the light of life. - John 8: 12

By following the light of the world (Jesus), we will never get lost and lose our way.

More From A Patriot's Guide

Thanks for reading this guide. We hope you enjoyed it and will continue to read our other guides in the series. Here are a few of those:

Print Editions
- Christian Prayer - Prayer Tips From The Bible
- Christianity - It's Not What The World Thinks It Is!
- Deciphering The Man Code
- Exodus - An EZ Illustrated Commentary Of The Book Of Exodus
- Genesis - An EZ Illustrated Commentary Of The Book Of Genesis
- Revelation - An EZ Illustrated Commentary Of The Book Of Revelation
- Marriage - Biblical Tips On How To Stay Married Longer
- Acts - An EZ Illustrated Commentary Of The Book Of Acts
- The Epistles Of Paul - An EZ Illustrated Commentary Of The Epistles Of Paul
- The General Epistles - An EZ Illustrated Commentary Of The General Epistles
- The Gospel - The Gospel According To Matthew, Mark, Luke And John

E-books
- Being The Dad That God Wants You To Be
- Healthy Eating Tips From The Bible
- Christian Prayer - Prayer Tips From The Bible
- Ephesians - An EZ Illustrated Commentary Of The Book Of Ephesians
- Christianity - It's Not What The World Thinks It Is!
- Colossians - An EZ Illustrated Commentary Of The Book Of

Visit our website if you would like to know more about A Patriot's Guide and the Author/Illustrator: **www.apatriotsguide.com**

Printed in Great Britain
by Amazon